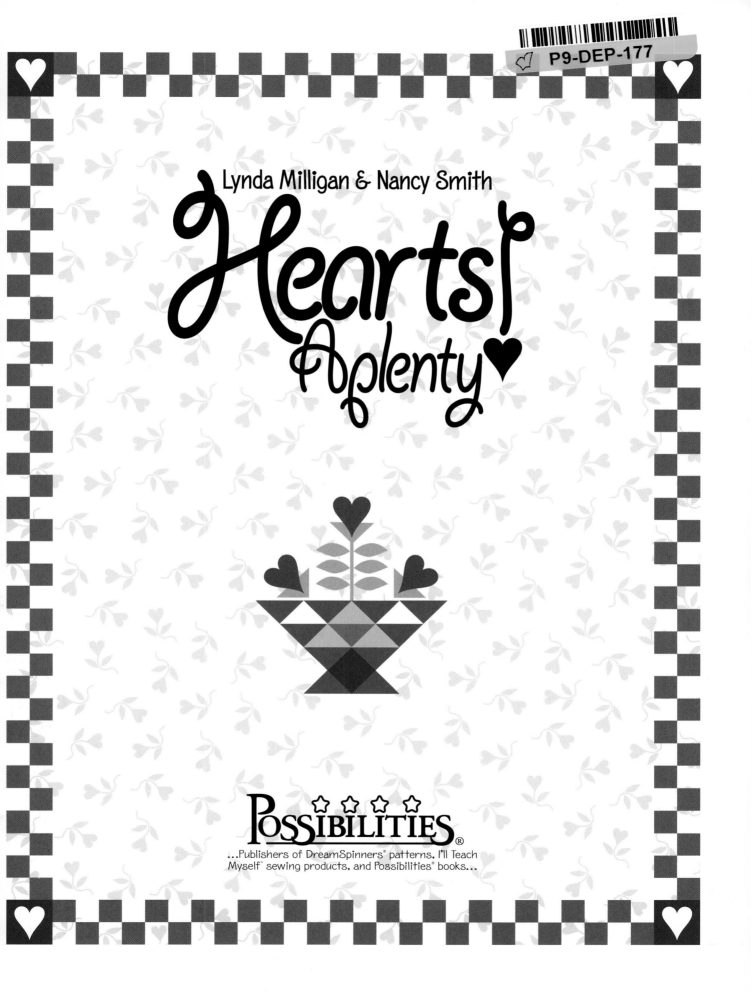

Lynda Milligan & Nancy Smith

Hearts Aplenty

POSSIBILITIES®
...Publishers of DreamSpinners® patterns, I'll Teach
Myself™ sewing products, and Possibilities® books...

Acknowledgements

We would like to dedicate this book to one of our most valuable friends and trusted employees, Judy Carpenter. If we have to name one person who has her finger on the pulse of our company, it would have to be Judy. She is the champion of all jugglers.

For seventeen years, Judy has given her all to both the retail and wholesale divisions of Great American Quilt Factory. She spends her days off and sleepless nights thinking about what changes can be made to better the business and how we can serve customers and make them feel warm and welcome. Judy has a knack for efficiency, cost-cutting avenues, and smooth-running operations. She is a loyal supporter, a visionary, and is confident in her skills as well as undaunted by new challenges. We are so lucky to have her.

It is with pride and appreciation that we dedicate this book to Judy.

Special Thanks

Jane Dumler, Joanne Malone, Jan Hagan, Ann Petersen, Michielle Schlichenmayer, Barbara O'Melia, Sharron Shimbel, Katie Wells, Susan Auskaps, Sharon Holmes, Courtenay Hughes, Eileen Lingen – For stitching & quilting
Sandi Fruehling, Susan F. Geddes, Carolyn Schmitt – For long-arm machine quilting

Crate & Barrel – for photography in their store

Pottery Barn for Kids – for props used in photography

Credits

Sharon Holmes – Editor, Technical Illustrator
Susan Johnson – Designer, Photo Stylist
Lexie Foster – Cover & Graphics, Designer, Photo Stylist
Lani Ho'a – Designer, Photo Stylist
Chris Scott – Editorial Assistant
Sandi Fruehling – Copy Reader
Brian Birlauf – Photographer
Lee Milne – Digital Photographer
Ernie Ho-a – Portrait Photographer

...Publishers of DreamSpinners® patterns, I'll Teach Myself™ sewing products, and Possibilities® books...

Hearts Aplenty

©2001 by Lynda Milligan & Nancy Smith

Published in the United States of America by Possibilities®, Denver, Colorado
Library of Congress Catalog Card Number: 2001088955
ISBN: 1-880972-44-1

Photo Index

APPLIQUE— Our favorite method of applique is the fusible web technique with a buttonhole stitch finish. Patterns are reversed and ready to be traced. Be sure to have plenty of fusible web on hand if using this method. Reverse and add seam allowance to patterns if doing hand applique.

Hearts Askew

For a beautiful baby quilt, use soft pastels or keep to a simple color scheme of blue and white for the squares and various shades of yellow for the hearts.

Photo on page 24

Approximate size 57 x 65" — 8" block

Use 42-45"-wide fabric. When strips appear in the cutting list, cut crossgrain strips (selvage to selvage).

YARDAGE

Backgrounds	¼ yd each of 10 or more blacks
	¼ yd each of 10 or more whites
Hearts	⅙ yd each of 6 or more reds & pinks
Border 1	½ yd black
Border 2	¾ yd bright pink
Binding	⅔ yd black
Backing	3¾ yd
Batting	63 x 71"

CUTTING

Center squares	21 light squares 6⅜"
	21 dark squares 6⅜"
Corners	42 light rectangles 3¾ x 6¼"
	42 dark rectangles 3¾ x 6¼"
Hearts	42 – Pattern on page 37 – See Step 3
Border 1	6 strips 2" wide
Border 2	6 strips 3½" wide
Binding	7 strips 2½" wide

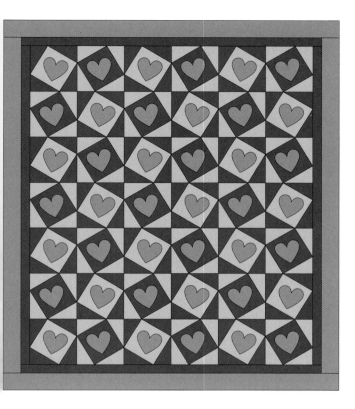

1. STACK all black rectangles RIGHT SIDE UP, then cut as shown.
STACK all white rectangles RIGHT SIDE UP, then cut as shown.

Blacks   Whites

2-3.

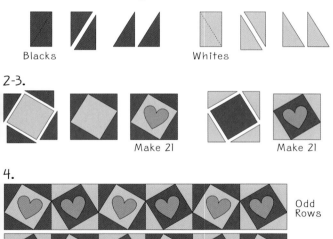

Make 21   Make 21

4.

Odd Rows

Even Rows

DIRECTIONS

Use ¼" seam allowance unless otherwise noted.

1. Stack all 3¾ x 6¼" black rectangles RIGHT SIDE UP. Cut all in HALF diagonally exactly as shown. Stack all 3¾ x 6¼" white rectangles RIGHT SIDE UP. Cut all in HALF diagonally exactly as shown.

2. Make 21 blocks with light centers and dark corners and 21 blocks with dark centers and light corners. See diagram.

   Hints: For accurate stitching, mark seam intersections on wrong side of each triangle and square, then pin through marks before stitching triangle to square. Put through machine with triangle on bottom next to feed-dog.

3. Applique hearts to blocks, tilted as desired, using your favorite method. Our favorite method is fusible web, and our patterns are set up for it—reversed for tracing and no seam allowances added.

4. Stitch blocks into 7 rows of 6 blocks each, alternating as shown.

5. Stitch rows together. Press.

6. Border 1: Measure length of quilt. Piece border strips to the measured length and stitch to sides of quilt. Repeat at top and bottom. Press.

7. Border 2: Repeat Step 6.

8. Piece backing horizontally to same size as batting. Layer and quilt as desired. Trim backing and batting even with top.

9. Stitch binding strips together end to end. Press in half lengthwise, wrong sides together. Bind quilt using ⅜" seam allowance.

Stitched with Love

Have you ever seen such a happy quilt? What a treat to make for a special friend or loved one. If you don't have a big collection of plaids, substitute bright florals, dots, and stripes.

Photo on page 29

Approximate size 53 x 69" — 4" block

Use 42-45"-wide fabric. When strips appear in the cutting list, cut crossgrain strips (selvage to selvage).

YARDAGE

Bright flannels	¼ yd each of 24 or more fabrics
Applique panels	½ yd yellow or orange
Appliques	bright flannel scraps
Border 1	⅓ yd yellow or orange
Border 2	1 yd bright blue
Binding	⅔ yd yellow or orange
Backing	3½ yd
Batting	59 x 75"
Fusible web	1 yd

CUTTING

Bright flannels	144 squares 4½"
Applique panels	4½ x 36½", 4½ x 20½", and 4½ x 28½" – See Step 1
Appliques	See patterns on pages 34-36 & Step 1
Border 1	6 strips 1" wide
Border 2	6 strips 4½" wide
Binding	7 strips 2½" wide

DIRECTIONS

Use ¼" seam allowance unless otherwise noted.

1. Applique panels, keeping applique pieces out of ¼" seam allowance. Applique hearts on 3 of the 4½" squares. Fusible web applique works best for flannel. Patterns are reversed for tracing and no seam allowances are added.

2. Lay out applique panels and squares, distributing colors as desired.

3. Stitch squares and applique panels into rows as shown.

4. Stitch rows together. Press.

5. Border 1: Measure length of quilt. Piece border strips to the measured length and stitch to sides of quilt. Repeat at top and bottom. Press.

6. Border 2: Repeat Step 5.

7. Piece backing horizontally to same size as batting. Layer and quilt as desired. Trim backing and batting even with top.

8. Stitch binding strips together end to end. Press in half lengthwise, wrong sides together. Bind quilt using ⅜" seam allowance.

1-3.

Love thy Neighbor

Celebrate a special family in your neighborhood or make this small quilt for a special friend and change the sentiment.

Photo on page 52

Approximate size 39 x 27"

Use 42-45"-wide fabric. When strips appear in the cutting list, cut crossgrain strips (selvage to selvage).

YARDAGE

Center panel	$\frac{2}{3}$ yd black
Snow	$\frac{1}{4}$ yd white
Appliques	$\frac{1}{4}$ yd purple for houses (1 or 2 fabrics)
	$\frac{1}{6}$ yd green stripe for roofs
	scraps from center panel fabric for lettering
	orange, red, & purple scraps or eighth yard pieces for hearts, lightning, & dog collars
	teal, blue, & lavender scraps for windows & doors
	green scraps for cat, dogs, chimneys
Border 1	$\frac{1}{8}$ yd red
Border 2	$\frac{1}{4}$ yd light purple
	$\frac{1}{4}$ yd dark purple
	$\frac{1}{6}$ yd purple solid (also Border 3)
Border 3	$\frac{5}{8}$ yd green
Binding	$\frac{3}{8}$ yd light purple
Backing	$1\frac{1}{2}$ yd
Batting	43 x 31"
Fusible web	2 yd

CUTTING

Center panel	30 x 18"
Snow	30 x 6" – See Step 1 before cutting
Appliques	See patterns on pages 38-40 & Step 5
Border 1	3 strips $\frac{3}{4}$" wide
Border 2	*4 dark purple squares $2\frac{3}{8}$"
	**7 dark purple squares $4\frac{1}{4}$"
	**8 light purple squares $4\frac{1}{4}$"
	4 purple solid squares 2"
Border 3	4 green strips $3\frac{1}{2}$" wide
	4 purple solid squares $3\frac{1}{2}$"
Binding	4 strips $2\frac{1}{2}$" wide

*Cut these squares in HALF diagonally
**Cut these squares in QUARTERS diagonally

1.

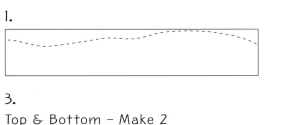

3.
Top & Bottom – Make 2

Sides – Make 2

DIRECTIONS

Use ¼" seam allowance unless otherwise noted.

1. Back the snow fabric with fusible web before cutting out the rectangle, then cut the top edge with a curvy line. Fuse to center panel, matching bottom and side edges.

2. Border 1: Measure length of quilt. Cut border strips to the measured length and stitch to sides of quilt. Repeat at top and bottom. Press.

3. Border 2: Make 2 side and 2 top/bottom borders with the dark and light purple triangles and the purple solid squares. The triangles cut from the 2⅜" squares go on the ends of each border. See diagram.

4. Border 3: Measure width and length of quilt. Cut border strips to the measured length and stitch to sides of quilt. Cut border strips to the measured width of quilt for top and bottom borders. Stitch purple solid squares to ends of each border and stitch borders to quilt. Press.

5. Applique the center panel. Our favorite method of applique is fusible web, and our patterns are set up for it—reversed for tracing and no seam allowances added.

6. Cut backing to same size as batting. Layer and quilt as desired. Trim backing and batting even with top.

7. Stitch binding strips together end to end. Press in half lengthwise, wrong sides together. Bind quilt using ⅜" seam allowance.

Love is all Around

Photo on page 53

Approximate size 62 x 78" — 8" block

Use 42-45"-wide fabric. When strips appear in the cutting list, cut crossgrain strips (selvage to selvage).

YARDAGE
Pattern A	⅓ yd each of 12 greens, golds
Pattern B	¼ yd each of 12 or more reds, purples, greens, golds
Arcs	⅛ yd each of 50 or more reds, purples, greens, golds
Hearts	⅙ yd each of 6 or more reds, purples, fuchsias
Border 1	⅜ yd fuchsia
Border 2	1⅓ yd dark green
	¼ yd purple for corner squares
Binding	¾ yd purple
Backing	4 yd
Batting	68 x 84"

CUTTING
Pattern A fabrics	4 of each fabric – Pattern A – Page 44
Pattern B fabrics	48 Pattern B – Page 44
Arc fabric	1 strip 3" wide of each fabric
Hearts	20 or more – Patterns on page 46 – See Step 5
Border 1	6 strips 1½" wide
Border 2	6 strips 6½" wide
	4 squares 6½"
Binding	8 strips 2½" wide

We love making scrap quilts with lots of fabrics from our stash. When it comes time to give yardage in our books, we try to make sure there are enough fabrics to create the scrappy look of the original without making buying the yardage unreasonable. Have a fabric exchange with a group of friends to increase your scrap stash.

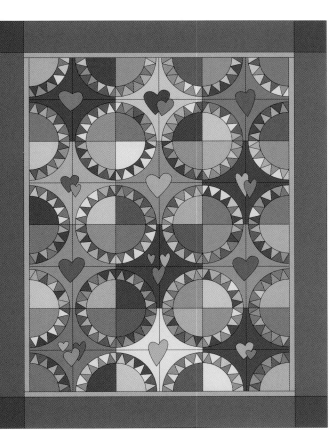

DIRECTIONS

Use ¼" seam allowance unless otherwise noted.

1. Paper piece 48 arcs using pieces cut from 3" strips. Arc pattern is on page 45.

2. Make 48 blocks with arcs and pieces cut with Patterns A and B. Press.

3. Stitch blocks into 12 units of 4 blocks each, rotating blocks as shown and using the same fabric in the Pattern A position.

4. Stitch units into 4 rows of 3. Stitch rows together. Press.

5. Applique hearts to areas between blocks as shown, using your favorite method. Our favorite method is fusible web, and our patterns are set up for it—reversed for tracing and no seam allowances added.

6. Border 1: Measure length of quilt. Piece border strips to the measured length and stitch to sides of quilt. Repeat at top and bottom. Press.

7. Border 2: Measure length and width of quilt. Piece border strips to the measured length for sides of quilt. Stitch side borders to quilt. Piece border strips to the measured width for top and bottom of quilt. Stitch corner squares to top and bottom borders. Stitch borders to quilt.

8. Piece backing horizontally to same size as batting. Layer and quilt as desired. Trim backing and batting even with top.

9. Stitch binding strips together end to end. Press in half lengthwise, wrong sides together. Bind quilt using ⅜" seam allowance.

1.

Paper
piece
arc

2.

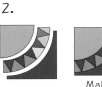

Make
48

3.

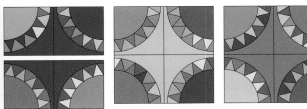

Cinnamon Hearts

Two similar blocks are used together in this pretty quilt to create an unusual design that looks like stars and chains.

Photo on page 32

Approximate size 60 x 78" — 9" block

Use 42-45"-wide fabric. When strips appear in the cutting list, cut crossgrain strips (selvage to selvage).

Yardage is figured for using pattern pieces for the side unit. If using the optional paper piecing pattern, more yardage may be needed for fabrics 1-3.

YARDAGE

Dark peach – #1	2¾ yd
Cream – #2	2 yd – includes Border 1
Light peach – #3	1¾ yd
Lavender – #4	⅞ yd
Light green – #5	1½ yd – includes Border 2
Medium green – #6	¾ yd
Light peachy pink	⅙ yd
Medium peachy pink	⅙ yd
Binding	¾ yd lavender
Backing	4 yd
Batting	66 x 84"

CUTTING

Dark peach – #1	164 Pattern A – page 43
	*48 squares 3⅞"
Cream – #2	7 strips 1½" wide – Border 1
	17 squares 3½"
	82 Pattern B, 82 Pattern B reversed – page 43
Light peach – #3	18 squares 3½"
	82 Pattern B, 82 Pattern B reversed – page 43
Lavender – #4	10 strips 2" wide
Light green – #5	10 strips 2" wide
	7 strips 3½" wide – Border 2
Medium green – #6	*48 squares 3⅞"
Appliques	18 light peachy pink
	17 medium peachy pink
	See patterns on page 43 & Step 3
Binding	7-8 strips 2½" wide

*Cut these squares in HALF diagonally

DIRECTIONS

Use ¼" seam allowance unless otherwise noted.

1. Make 18 Block A. Use pattern pieces A and B or optional paper piecing pattern on page 43. Fabrics are numbered in parentheses on diagram. Press.

2. Make 17 Block B: Make 10 strip sets with fabrics #4 and #5. Crosscut into 2" segments. Make four-patch units from segments. Finish blocks as shown. Press.

3. Applique hearts to blocks. Use light peachy pink for Block A and medium peachy pink for Block B. Our favorite method of applique is fusible web, and our patterns are set up for it—reversed for tracing and no seam allowances added.

4. Finishing Row: Make 10 Partial Block A and 14 Partial Block B as shown. Press.

5. Lay out blocks, alternating A and B. Lay out Partial Blocks around edges, placing carefully to finish large "shield shapes" around stars. Place four remaining half-square triangle units from Step 4 at corners. Stitch into horizontal rows as shown. Stitch rows together. Press.

6. Border 1: Measure length of quilt. Cut border strips to the measured length and stitch to sides of quilt. Repeat at top and bottom. Press.

7. Border 2: Repeat Step 6.

8. Piece backing horizontally to same size as batting. Layer and quilt as desired. Trim backing and batting even with top.

9. Stitch binding strips together end to end. Press in half lengthwise, wrong sides together. Bind quilt using ⅜" seam allowance.

1.
For one Block A:

Make 4 (#1, #6)

Make 4 (#1, #2)

(#3 center)

Make 18

2. For one Block B:

Make 10 (#4, #5)

Make 4

Make 4 (#1, #3)

(#2 center)

Make 17

4. Finishing Row

Make 24 (#1, #6)

Make 28 (#4, #5)

Make 14 (#1, #3)

Make 10 (#1, #2)

Make 10 Partial Block A

Make 14 Partial Block B

5.

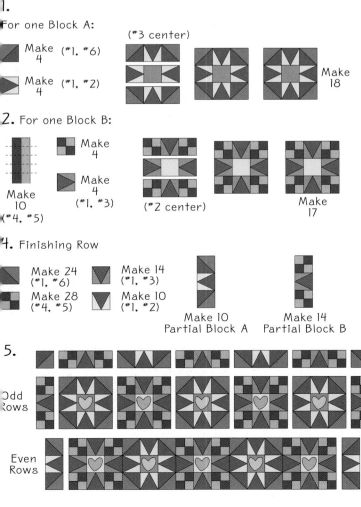

Odd Rows

Even Rows

Loves Me, Loves Me Not

A striking quilt in black, white, and red, Loves Me, Loves Me Not would be equally beautiful with yellow flowers and a blue and white border. A pastel version would be lovely also.

Photo on page 17

Approximate size 44 x 56"

Use 42-45"-wide fabric. When strips appear in the cutting list, cut crossgrain strips (selvage to selvage).

YARDAGE

Center panel	⅞ yd black
Appliques	⅙ yd each of 2-4 reds, 2-4 oranges
	⅛ yd each of 2-4 yellows, 6-8 dark greens, 4-6 light greens
	⅜ yd dark green for stems
Border 1 & binding	1¼ yd red
Border 2	⅙ yd each of 8 or more black prints
	⅙ yd each of 8 or more white prints
Backing	3 yd
Batting	48 x 60"
Fusible web	1½ yd

CUTTING

Center panel	22½ x 34½"
Appliques	See patterns on pages 41-42 & Step 2
Border 1	4 strips 1½" wide
Border 2	78 black squares 3½"
	78 white squares 3½"
Binding	5-6 strips 5" wide (finishes 1" wide)

DIRECTIONS

Use ¼" seam allowance unless otherwise noted.

1. Border 1: Cut border strips 34½" long and stitch to sides of center panel. Cut border strips 24½" long and stitch to top and bottom of center panel. Press.

2. Applique:
Use of a nonstick applique pressing sheet is recommended.

   a. Vase: Copy vase pattern on page 41 to lightweight paper. Using light greens, paper piece from top to bottom, sewing on dashed lines, and covering paper past gray line. Cut out on gray line. Remove paper. From book, trace black and gray lines of vase to fusible web, then cut out fusible web halfway between the two lines. Fuse to wrong side of vase. Cut out vase on black line. Trace vase top to fusible web and fuse to wrong side of yellow or orange fabric. Cut out on black line.

   b. Flowers: Make 3 copies of page 42 on lightweight paper. Using black for centers and yellows and oranges for edges, paper piece eight flower centers, covering paper past gray line. Cut out on gray line. Remove paper. From book, trace black and gray lines of flower centers to fusible web, then cut out fusible web halfway between the two lines. Fuse web piece to wrong side of each flower center. Cut out on black line. Trace 8 flowers to fusible web. Fuse to back of red and orange fabrics and cut out. Fuse prepared flower centers to flowers using the nonstick applique pressing sheet. Trace 14 extra petals to fusible web and fuse to back of red and orange fabrics.

   c. Leaves: Cut 1⅛ x 15" and ⅞ x 15" strips of dark greens. Piece into 10 x 15" rectangle. Press. Cut a 9½ x 14½" rectangle of fusible web. Trace 34 leaves to this piece of fusible web, tilting different directions. Press fusible web to back of pieced rectangle. Cut out leaves.

   d. Stems: Cut a 12 x 18" rectangle of dark green fabric and a 11½ x 17½" rectangle of fusible web. Fuse web to wrong side of fabric. Cut 8-10 bias strips ¼" wide.

3a-b.

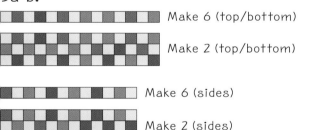

Make 6 (top/bottom)

Make 2 (top/bottom)

Make 6 (sides)

Make 2 (sides)

3c.

Continued on page 16.

LOVES ME, LOVES ME NOT

Continued from page 15.

> e. Remove paper backing from appliques. Arrange and fuse appliques to center panel using photo and diagram as guides. Stem pieces will curve as needed. Save some single petals to fuse to patchwork border later.

3. Border 2:

   a. Stitch 6 rows of 14, alternating black and white squares as shown for top and bottom borders. Stitch rows together, rotating center row to create checkerboard effect. Press.

   b. Repeat for side borders, alternating 12 squares in each row. Press.

   c. Stitch side border units to quilt, then top and bottom border units. See diagram for proper rotation of units. Press.

   d. Applique remaining single flower petals to bottom border.

4. Piece backing horizontally to same size as batting. Layer and quilt as desired. We used horizontal quilting lines to simulate a table top and vertical quilting lines in the upper background behind the vase. Trim backing and batting ¾" from edge of quilt top (so there will be batting inside the wide binding).

5. One-inch binding:

   a. Stitch binding strips together end to end to fit each side of quilt plus 3" extra. Press in half lengthwise, wrong sides together.

   b. Bind sides first. Beginning at edge of backing/batting, pin raw edges of binding even with raw edge of quilt top. Trim binding even with backing/batting at each end. Stitch with ¼" seam allowance. Fold binding over raw edge so that fold meets stitched line on backing. Pin. Stitch to backing by hand.

   c. Repeat for top and bottom of quilt. Allow binding to extend ¾" at both ends. Turn extended portion of binding in, then finish hand stitching binding to back of quilt as in Step b.

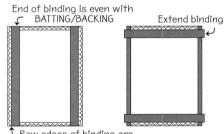

End of binding is even with BATTING/BACKING

Extend binding

Raw edges of binding are even with raw edge of QUILT TOP

Quilt Label See directions for use on page 65.

This quilt was especially handcrafted for:

With much affection by:

DATE: PLACE:

16

Love Blooms

Photo on page 49

Approximate size 43 x 54" — 9" block

Use 42-45"-wide fabric. When strips appear in the cutting list, cut crossgrain strips (selvage to selvage).

Wouldn't this quilt look lovely on a summer porch with white wicker furniture. For a fun kid's quilt, the beautiful florals could be changed to bright geometric prints.

YARDAGE

Blocks	⅔ yd for background
	⅛ yd each of 8-12 florals for side units & centers
	⅛ yd each of 6-12 greens for corners
Frames & Border 1	¾ yd black
Sashing rectangles	⅔ yd black & white stripe
Sashing squares	⅛ yd floral
Border 2	¼ yd pink
Border 3	¾ yd floral
Binding	½ yd floral
Backing	3 yd
Batting	47 x 58"

CUTTING

Blocks	**24 squares 4¼" background
	48 squares 2" background
	12 squares 3½" – florals – for center
	48 rectangles 2 x 3½" – florals – for side units
	*48 squares 2⅜" – florals – for side units
	48 squares 2" – greens – for corners
	*48 squares 2⅜" – greens – for corners
Frames	12 strips 1" wide
Sashing rectangles	31 rectangles 1½ x 10½"
Sashing squares	20 squares 1½"
Border 1	5 strips 1½" wide
Border 2	5 strips 1" wide
Border 3	5 strips 3½" wide
Binding	5 strips 2½" wide

*Cut these squares in HALF diagonally
**Cut these squares in QUARTERS diagonally

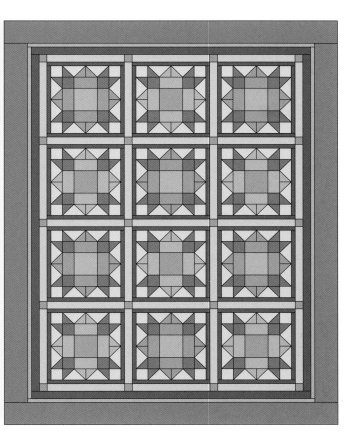

DIRECTIONS

Use ¼″ seam allowance unless otherwise noted.

1. Make 12 blocks with frames following diagram. Mix florals for centers and side units as desired. Press.
2. Make 5 rows of sashing squares and rectangles. Make 4 rows of 3 blocks and 4 sashing rectangles. See diagram.
3. Stitch alternating rows of blocks and sashing together. Press.
4. Border 1: Measure length of quilt. Piece border strips to the measured length and stitch to sides of quilt. Repeat at top and bottom. Press.
5. Borders 2 & 3: Repeat Step 4.
6. Piece backing horizontally to same size as batting. Layer and quilt as desired. Trim backing and batting even with top.
7. Stitch binding strips together end to end. Press in half lengthwise, wrong sides together. Bind quilt using ⅜″ seam allowance.

1.

For each block:

Make 4   Make 4

Make 2

Make 1

Make 2

2.

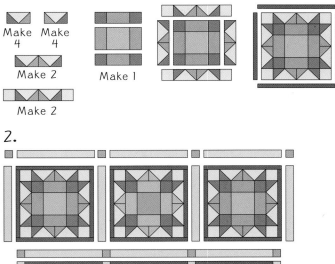

Blue Velvet – Page 22   Blue Velvet Pillows – Page 33

Blue Velvet

Fill all or some of the pretty baskets on this quilt with the flowers that are appliqued on the pillows—directions on page 33. Mix and match the applique pieces to make your own blooming bouquets.

If you have never paper-pieced half-square triangle units, this would be a great quilt for trying it. Check your local quilt store for Thangles® or Triangles on a Roll. The units finish at 2". With a short demonstration, you will be hooked! Note: Extra yardage may be needed for paper piecing.

Photo on page 20

Approximate size 78 x 95" — 12" block

Use 42-45"-wide fabric. When strips appear in the cutting list, cut crossgrain strips (selvage to selvage).

YARDAGE

Navy	6¾ yd for background & Border 2
Medium blue	1⅔ yd for baskets
Light blue	1 yd for baskets & Border 1
Binding	⅞ yd
Backing	7½ yd
Batting	84 x 101"

CUTTING

Navy	blocks	40 squares 2½"
		*100 squares 2⅞"
		*10 squares 8⅞"
		40 rectangles 2½ x 8½"
	setting squares	12 squares 12½"
	side setting triangles	**4 squares 18¼"
	corner setting triangles	*2 squares 9⅜"
	Border 2	9 strips 4½" wide
Medium blue		
	blocks	*10 squares 4⅞"
		*160 squares 2⅞"
Light blue		
	blocks	20 squares 2½"
		*40 squares 2⅞"
	Border 1	8-9 strips 1½" wide
Binding		9 strips 2½" wide

*Cut these squares in HALF diagonally
**Cut these squares in QUARTERS diagonally

DIRECTIONS

Use ¼" seam allowance unless otherwise noted.

1. Make 20 blocks following diagram. Press.

2. Lay out blocks, setting squares, and setting triangles. Stitch into diagonal rows. Stitch rows together.

3. Border 1: Measure length of quilt. Piece border strips to the measured length and stitch to sides of quilt. Repeat at top and bottom. Press.

4. Border 2: Repeat Step 4.

5. Piece backing horizontally to same size as batting. Layer and quilt as desired. Trim backing and batting even with top.

6. Stitch binding strips together end to end. Press in half lengthwise, wrong sides together. Bind quilt using ⅜" seam allowance.

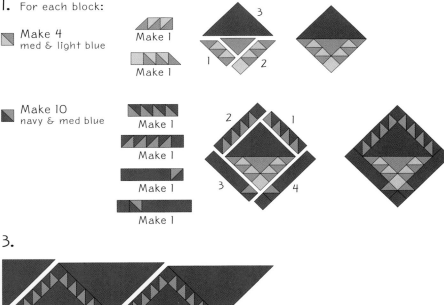

1. For each block:

Make 4
med & light blue
Make 1
Make 1

Make 10
navy & med blue
Make 1
Make 1
Make 1
Make 1

3.

Hearts Askew – Page 4   Conversation Hearts – Page 78   Chenille Rug – Page 77

Simply Hearts – Page 58   Plate Charmers & Plate Mats – Page 79

Don't Fence Me in

We set these Rail Fence blocks together in a woven pattern rather than in the traditional way.

The pillow in the photo on page 21 was made with the 3″ patchwork heart block from Home Is Where the Heart Is, page 74. For a 14″ pillow form, make 9 blocks for the center. Add a 1/2″ (finished width) border, then a 2″ (finished width) border with corner squares. Piping or a bound seam at the outside edge completes the look.

Photo on page 21   Approximate size 78 x 87″

4½″ Rail Fence block, 8½″ Log Cabin block, 8½″ heart block

Use 42-45″-wide fabric. When strips appear in the cutting list, cut crossgrain strips (selvage to selvage).

NOTE: Since this quilt has a patchwork border, precise piecing of all elements is critical. Rail Fence blocks should measure 5″ raw edge to raw edge. Heart and Log Cabin blocks should measure 9″ raw edge to raw edge. Border 1 is cut a different width for the sides than it is for the top and bottom so the heart/Log Cabin border will fit.

YARDAGE

Rail Fence & Log Cabin blocks	⅝ yd each of reds #1, #2, #3
	½ yd each of reds #4, #5, #6
	⅜ yd each of reds #7, #8, #9
	½ yd each of reds #10, #11, #12
	⅜ yd each of reds #13, #14, #15
Heart blocks	½ yd each of 3 reds for right side (strip set)
	⅝ yd red for upper left corner
	⅞ yd purple for lower background
	½ yd purple for upper background
Border 1 & 3	¾ yd fuchsia
Border 4	1½ yd purple
Binding	⅞ yd fuchsia
Backing	7⅜ yd
Batting	84 x 93″

CUTTING

Rail Fence blocks	6 strips each of reds #1, #2, #3 – 2″ wide – Set A
	4 strips each of reds #4, #5, #6 – 2″ wide – Set B
	3 strips each of reds #7, #8, #9 – 2″ wide – Set C
	4 strips each of reds #10, #11, #12 – 2″ wide – Set D
	3 strips each of reds #13, #14, #15 – 2″ wide – Set E
Log Cabin blocks	4 squares 3″ – red – for centers
	2 strips 1½″ wide of each of 5 reds & 1 purple
Heart blocks	6 strips 2″ wide of each fabric for right side
	26 rectangles 3½ x 5″ of upper left corner fabric
	*26 squares 5⅛″ of lower background fabric
	*26 squares 3″ of upper background fabric
	**7 squares 5½″ of upper background fabric
Border 1	4 strips 1¼″ wide for sides
	3 strips 1″ wide for top & bottom
Border 3	8 strips 1¼″ wide
Border 4	8-9 strips 5″ wide
Binding	9 strips 2½″ wide

*Cut these squares in HALF diagonally
**Cut these squares in QUARTERS diagonally

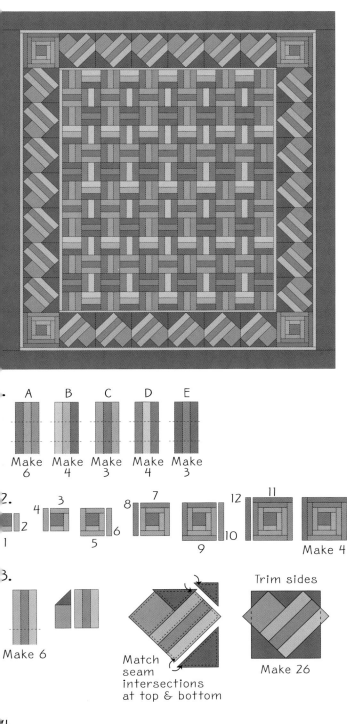

DIRECTIONS

Use ¼" seam allowance unless otherwise noted.

1. Rail Fence Blocks: Make Strip Sets A–E using cutting chart and diagrams as guides. Crosscut into 5" segments. Label piles of blocks with letter names. Set aside.

2. Log Cabin Blocks: Using fabrics as desired, stitch strips around center square in counterclockwise order as shown. Trim ends of strips away as you sew. Set aside.

3. Heart Blocks

   a. Make 6 strip sets with 2" strips. Press. Crosscut into 8" segments.

   b. Stitch a 3½x5" rectangle to a triangle cut from the 5½" squares. See diagram. Stitch this unit to one of the 8" segments.

   c. Matching seam intersections at top edge of block, stitch triangles cut from 3" squares to block. Sides of heart will extend. Repeat at bottom of block with triangles cut from 5⅛" squares. See diagram. Press.

   d. Trim excess on sides of block.

4. Lay out Rail Fence blocks in rows as shown. Stitch blocks into rows. Stitch rows together. Press.

5. Border 1: Measure length of quilt. Piece 1¼" side border strips to the measured length and stitch to sides of quilt. Repeat at top and bottom with 1" strips. Press.

6. Border 2: Stitch 7 heart blocks each into borders for sides. Stitch to sides of quilt. Stitch 6 heart blocks and 2 Log Cabin blocks into border for top. Repeat for bottom. Stitch top and bottom borders to quilt. Press.

7. Borders 3 & 4: Measure length of quilt. Piece border strips to the measured length and stitch to sides of quilt. Repeat at top and bottom. Press.

8. Piece backing horizontally to same size as batting. Layer and quilt as desired. Trim backing and batting even with top.

9. Stitch binding strips together end to end. Press in half lengthwise, wrong sides together. Bind using ⅜" seam allowance.

Heartbeats – Page 70   Heartbeats Wall Hanging – Page 72

A QUILT STITCHED WITH THE THREAD OF LOVE IS COMFORT FOR THE SOUL

Sealed with a Kiss

Photo on page 57

Approximate size 52 x 64" — 4½ x 6½" block

Use 42-45"-wide fabric. When strips appear in the cutting list, cut crossgrain strips (selvage to selvage).

The possibilities for this quilt are endless. Make a smaller quilt with 24 blocks for a great advent calendar. Place small treats in the envelopes. For a friend who is under the weather, tuck in special get-well messages. It would also be fun to put small school mementos and pictures in the envelopes for children. If you don't want to make the buttonholes, use clear snaps instead or just leave the flap alone.

YARDAGE

Envelope blocks	½ yd each of 15 or more bright prints
Sashing rectangles	1 yd black
Sashing/Border 2 squares	¼ yd black & white check
Border 1	½ yd lime green
Border 2	⅜ yd black with white dots
Border 3	1 yd bright blue
Binding	⅔ yd bright blue
Backing	3⅜ yd
Batting	56 x 68"
Buttons	45

CUTTING

Envelope blocks	45 rectangles 5 x 7" for backs
	90 squares 5½" for sides
	45 rectangles 3¾ x 7" for flaps
Sashing rectangles	54 rectangles 1½ x 5"
	50 rectangles 1½ x 7"
Sashing/Border 2 squares	64 squares 1½"
Border 1	5 strips 2½" wide
Border 2	5 strips 1½" wide
Border 3	6 strips 4½" wide
Binding	6-7 strips 2½" wide

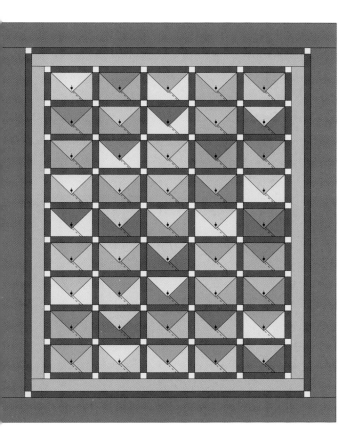

DIRECTIONS

Use ¼″ seam allowance unless otherwise noted.

1. Envelope blocks – Make 45

   a. Press 2 side pieces in half diagonally, wrong sides together. Pin to right side of block back piece, bottom corners matching. Points extend at top.

   b. Pin side pieces together at overlap. Remove sides from back and stitch close to edge along diagonal overlap.

   c. Place sides on back piece again. Stitch side and bottom edges together ⅛″ from edge, as shown.

   d. Fold flap piece in half, right sides together, to a 3½ x 3¾″ rectangle. Stitch one 3½″ edge. See diagram. Trim point. Turn right side out and place seam in center as shown. Press.

   e. Pin flap to top edge of envelope block, raw edges even, and stitch ⅛″ from edge.

   f. Make buttonhole in point of flap and sew button to side pieces directly beneath.

2. Make 10 rows of sashing rectangles and sashing squares as shown. Make 9 rows of blocks and sashing rectangles as shown.

3. Stitch rows of sashing and rows of blocks together. Press.

4. Border 1: Measure length of quilt. Piece border strips to the measured length and stitch to sides of quilt. Repeat at top and bottom. Press.

5. Border 2: Measure length and width of quilt. Piece border strips to the measured length for sides of quilt. Stitch side borders to quilt. Piece border strips to the measured width for top and bottom of quilt. Stitch corner squares to top and bottom borders. Stitch borders to quilt.

6. Border 3: Repeat Step 4.

7. Piece backing horizontally to same size as batting. Layer and quilt as desired. Trim backing and batting even with top.

8. Stitch binding strips together end to end. Press in half lengthwise, wrong sides together. Bind quilt using ⅜″ seam allowance.

a-c.

d.

Trim

e-f.

2.

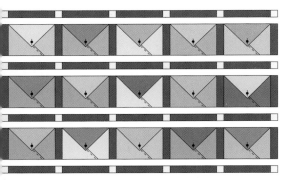

31

BLUE VELVET PILLOWS

Photo on page 20

Size 20" — 12" block

Use 42-45"-wide fabric. When strips appear in the cutting list, cut crossgrain strips (selvage to selvage).

YARDAGE For one pillow

Navy	⅓ yd for background
Medium blue	¼ yd for basket
Light blue	⅛ yd for basket
Appliques	scraps or eighth yards of 10 or more brights – Patterns on pages 47-48
Bright blue	½ yd for frame & binding
Black/blue stripe	½ yd for corners
Navy or dark blue	⅞ yd for border & envelope back

20" pillow form

Optional if quilting pillow top:

Batting	24" square
Backing	¾ yd

CUTTING For one pillow

Navy	2 squares 2½"
	*5 squares 2⅞"
	*1 square 8⅞"
	2 rectangles 2½ x 8½"
Medium blue	*1 square 4⅞"
	*8 squares 2⅞"
Light blue	1 square 2½"
	*2 squares 2⅞"
Appliques	Patterns on pages 47-48
Bright blue	2 strips ⅞" wide for frame
	2-3 strips 2½" wide for binding
Black/blue stripe	*2 squares 9⅞" (cut squares with stripe running corner to corner)
Navy or dark blue	2 strips 1½" wide
	2 rectangles 15 x 20½" for envelope back

*Cut these squares in HALF diagonally

DIRECTIONS

Use ¼" seam allowance unless otherwise noted.

1. Piece block, referring to Step 1, page 23. Applique block. Our favorite method of applique is fusible web, and our patterns are set up for it—reversed for tracing and no seam allowances added.

2. Stitch ⅞" strips to each side for frame. Press.

3. Stitch triangles cut from stripe to sides of block. Press.

4. Stitch 1½" border strips to each side. Press.

5. Optional: Cut backing for quilting to same size as batting. Layer and quilt as desired.

6. Envelope back: On one 20½" side of each backing rectangle, press 1" to wrong side, press 1" over again. Stitch hem close to fold. Lay backs on block, wrong sides of pillow backs against wrong side of pillow front, raw edges matching, hemmed edges overlapping at center of pillow. Baste entire outside edge.

7. Stitch binding strips together end to end. Press in half lengthwise, wrong sides together. Bind pillow using ⅜" seam allowance.

Stitched
with
Love

34

Patterns are reversed for tracing to fusible web

Stitched
with
Love

Cut 3

Patterns are reversed for
tracing to fusible web

35

Stitched
with
Love

Patterns are reversed for tracing to fusible web

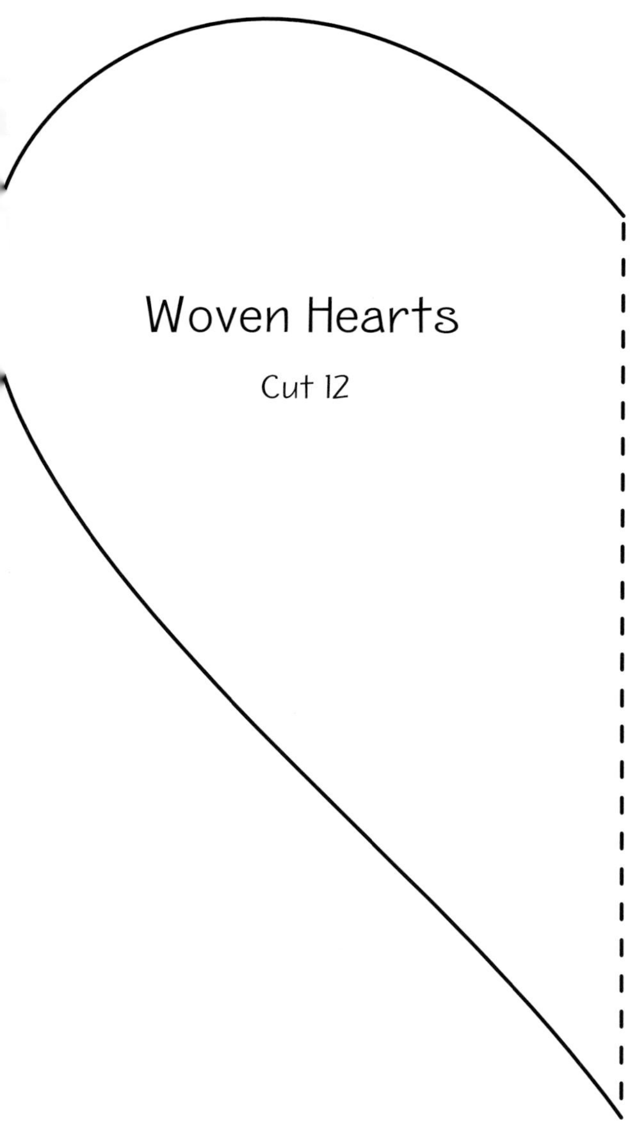

Woven Hearts

Cut 12

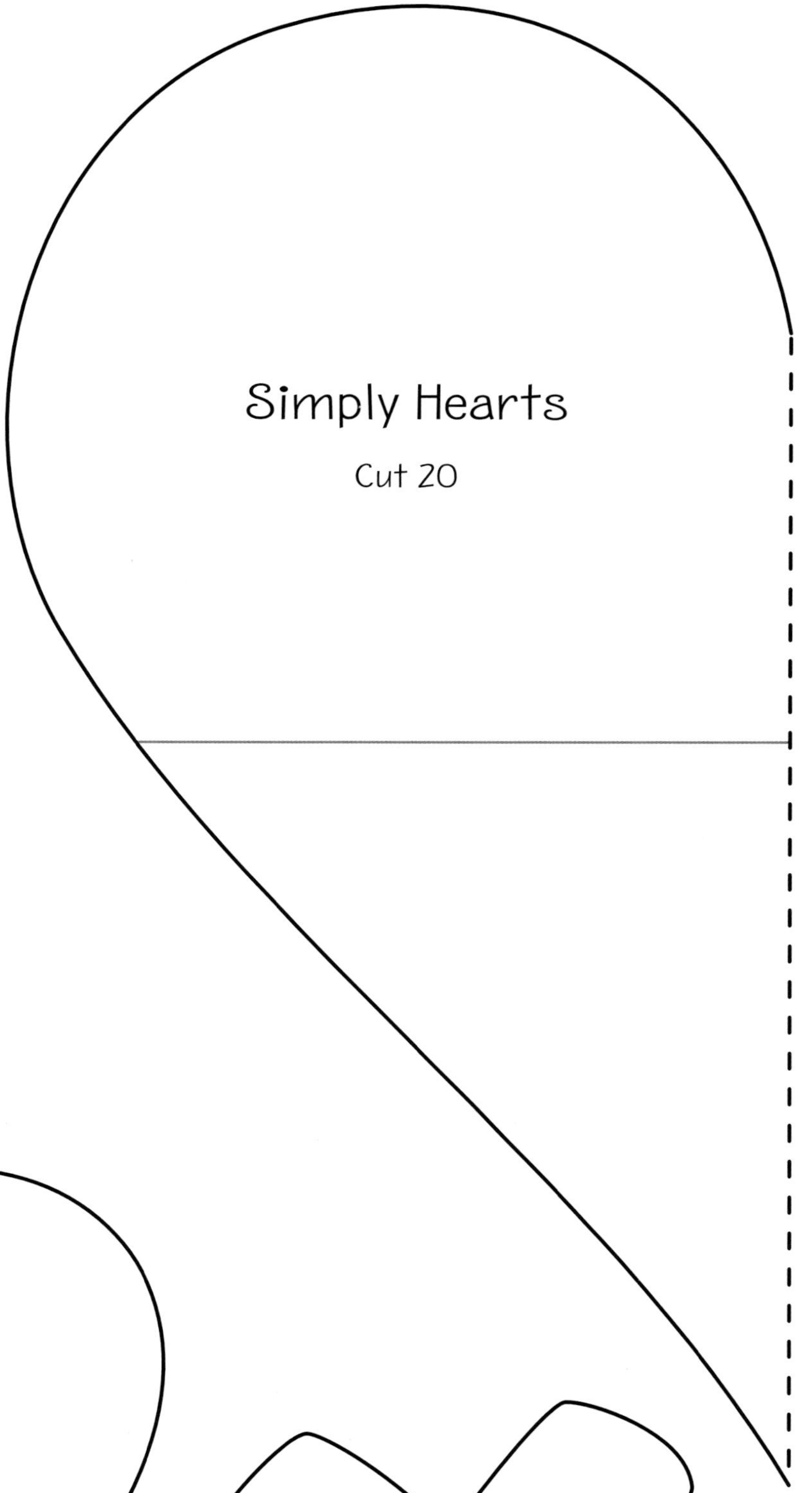

Simply Hearts

Cut 20

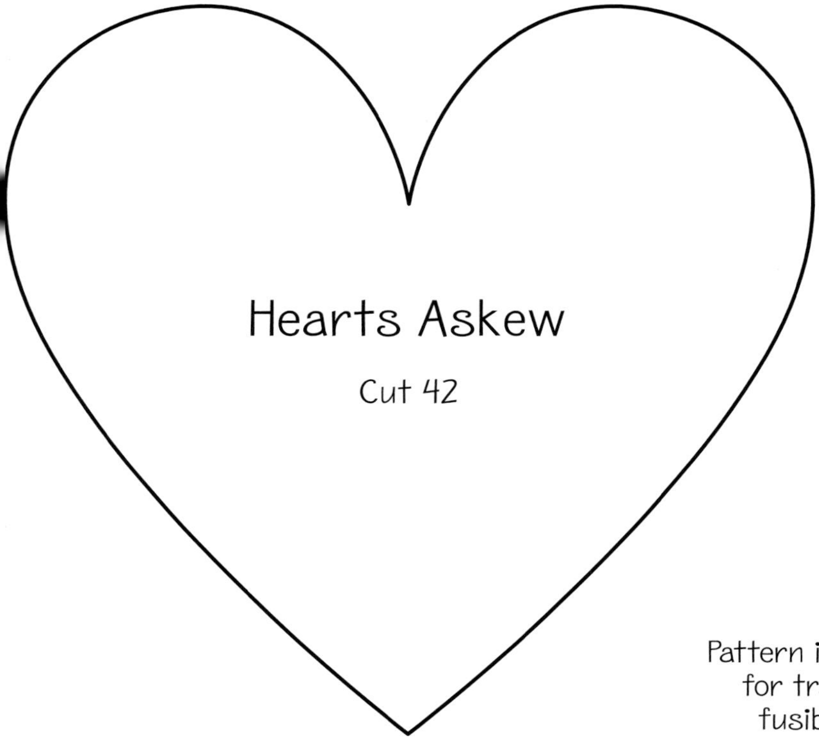

Hearts Askew

Cut 42

Crazy for You

Cut 4

Pattern is reversed
for tracing to
fusible web

Love thy Neighbor

Match to dotted line on page 39 for full pattern

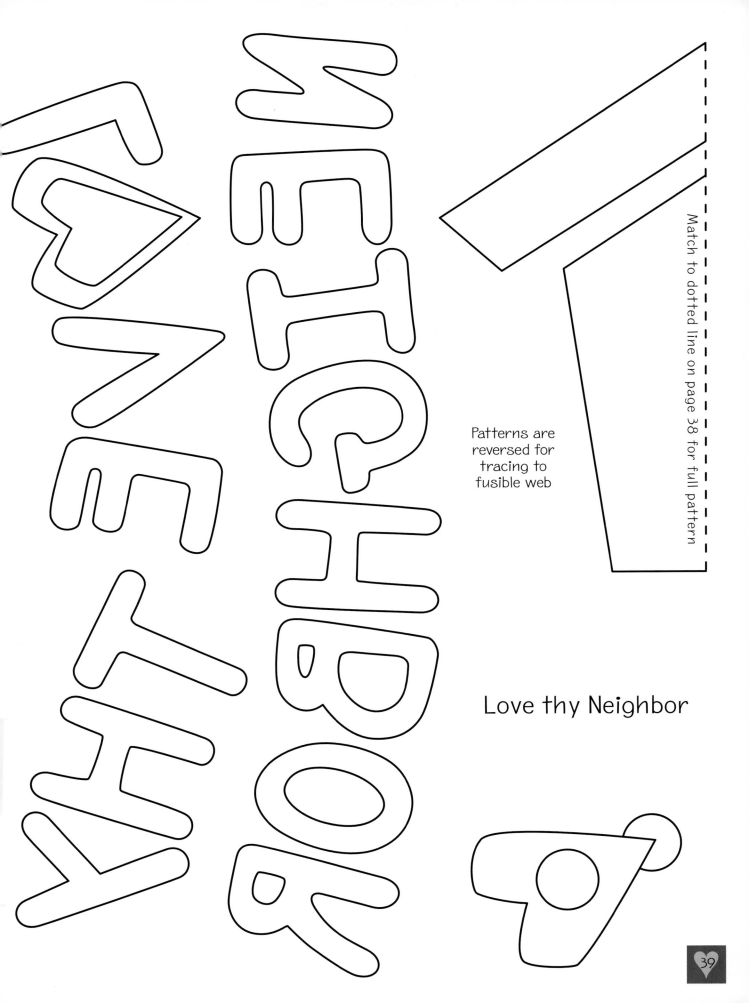

Match to dotted line on page 38 for full pattern

Patterns are
reversed for
tracing to
fusible web

Love thy Neighbor

Use also for
Plate Mat

Love
thy
Neighbor

Patterns are reversed for
tracing to fusible web

Loves Me,
Loves Me Not

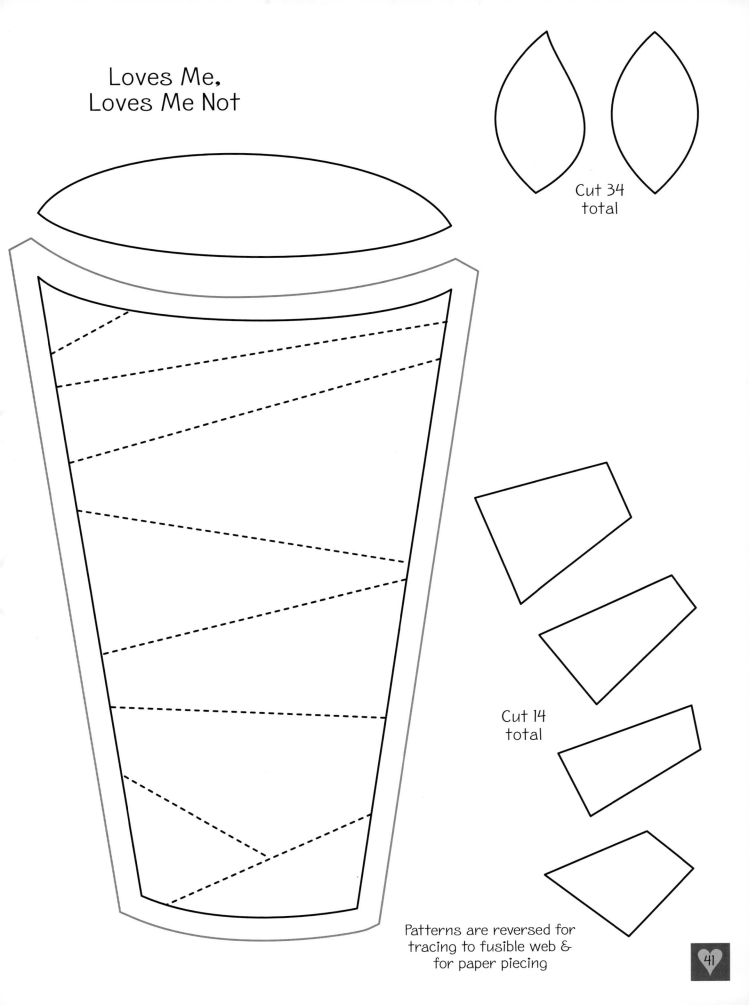

Cut 34
total

Cut 14
total

Patterns are reversed for
tracing to fusible web &
for paper piecing

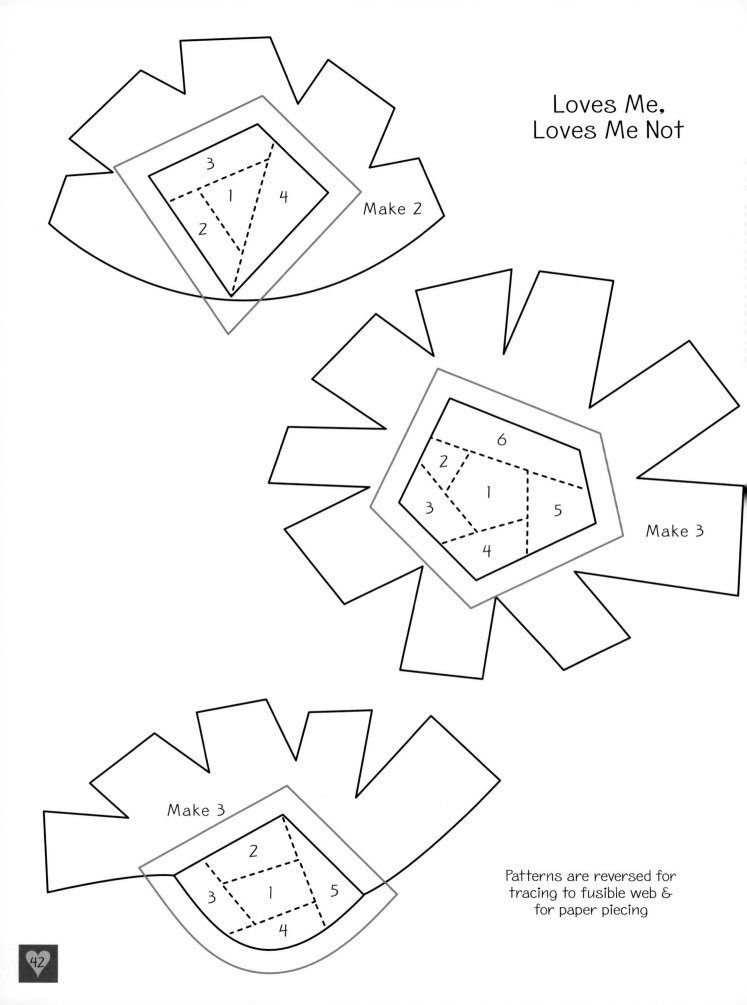

Loves Me,
Loves Me Not

Make 2

3
1   4
2

6
2
1
3   5
4

Make 3

Make 3

2
3   1   5
4

Patterns are reversed for
tracing to fusible web &
for paper piecing

42

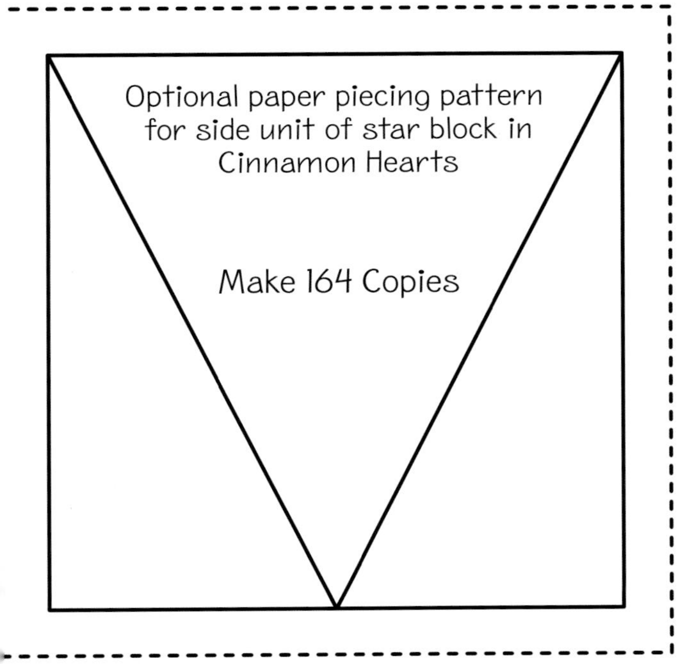

Optional paper piecing pattern for side unit of star block in Cinnamon Hearts

Make 164 Copies

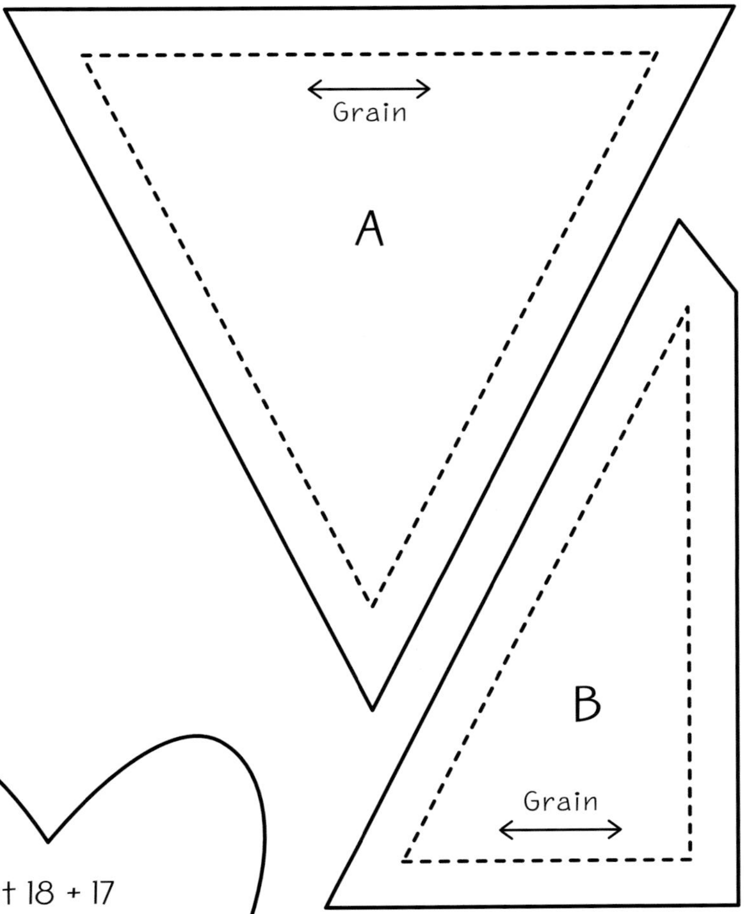

Grain ←→

A

B

Grain ←→

Cinnamon Hearts

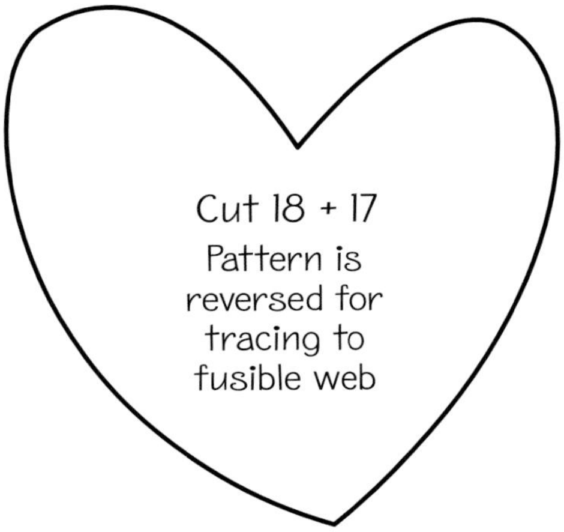

Cut 18 + 17
Pattern is reversed for tracing to fusible web

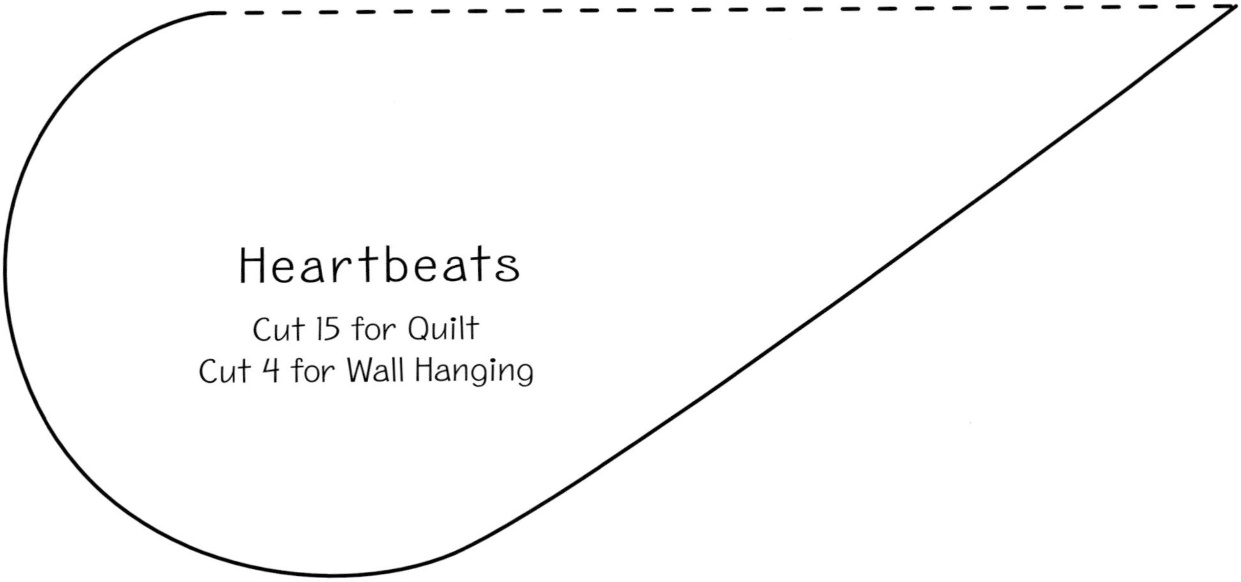

Heartbeats

Cut 15 for Quilt
Cut 4 for Wall Hanging

Love Is All Around

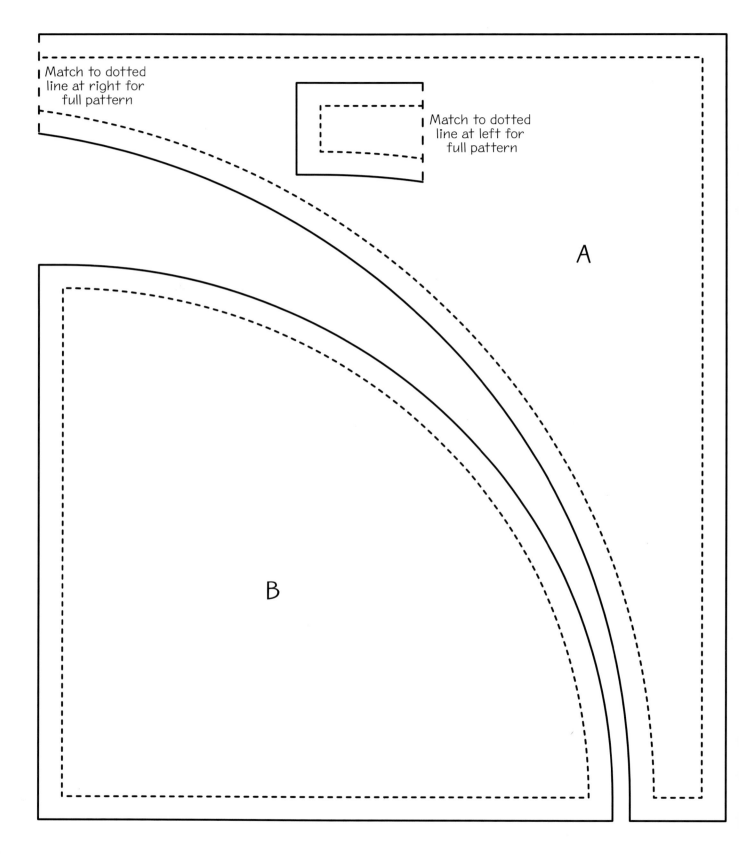

Match to dotted line at right for full pattern

Match to dotted line at left for full pattern

A

B

44

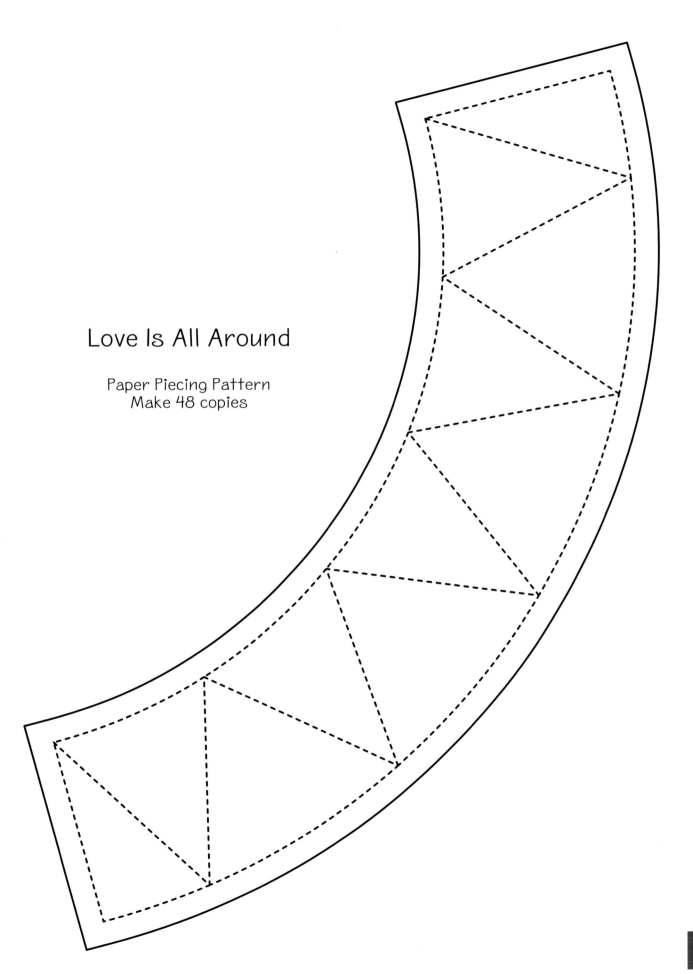

Love Is All Around

Paper Piecing Pattern
Make 48 copies

45

Patterns are reversed for
tracing to fusible web

Love Is
All Around

46

Blue Velvet Pillows

Patterns are reversed for
tracing to fusible web

Blue Velvet Pillows

Patterns are reversed for
tracing to fusible web

Love Blooms – Page 18

Alphabet Soup

To personalize this quilt even more, use rows 1, 7, 17, and 23 for information such as birth date and/or height and weight. Reduce the size of the letters to fit the narrower strips.

If you have never paper-pieced half-square triangle units, Rows 5, 12, and 19 would be great for trying it. Check your local quilt store for Thangles® or Triangles on a Roll. The units finish at 2". With a short demonstration, you will be hooked! Note: Extra yardage may be needed for paper piecing.

Photo on page 61

Approximate size 48 x 58"

Use 42-45"-wide fabric. When strips appear in the cutting list, cut crossgrain strips (selvage to selvage).

YARDAGE

Rows & appliques	1 yd dark green
	½ yd medium-dark green
	⅝ yd medium green
	1⅛ yd dark red
	⅞ yd medium red
	⅞ yd gold
	⅔ yd tan
	½ yd cream stripe
	¼ yd cream print
Binding	⅝ yd
Backing	3¼ yd
Batting	52 x 62"

CUTTING

Rows 1 & 23	3 strips 3½" – dark green
Rows 2 & 22	3 strips 1½" – medium green
Rows 3 & 21	3 strips 3⅜" – dark red
	3 strips 3⅜" – medium green
Rows 4 & 20	3 strips 5½" – gold
Row 5	*12 squares 2⅞" – gold
	*24 squares 2⅞" – dark green
	*12 squares 2⅞" – cream print
Rows 6, 8, 16, 18	5 strips 1½" – medium red
Rows 7 & 17	3 strips 3½" – medium-dark green
Rows 9, 11, 13, 15	5 strips 1½" – dark red
Row 10	2 strips 5½" – cream stripe
Row 12	*12 squares 2⅞" – cream print
	*24 squares 2⅞" – dark green
	*12 squares 2⅞" – tan
Row 14	2 strips 5½" – tan
Row 19	*12 squares 2⅞" – tan
	*24 squares 2⅞" – dark green
	*12 squares 2⅞" – gold
Appliques	Patterns on pages 91-94
	name – medium red
	8 hearts – medium red
	10 hearts – dark red
	5 Xs, 6 Os – dark red
Binding	6 strips 2½" wide

*Cut these squares in HALF diagonally

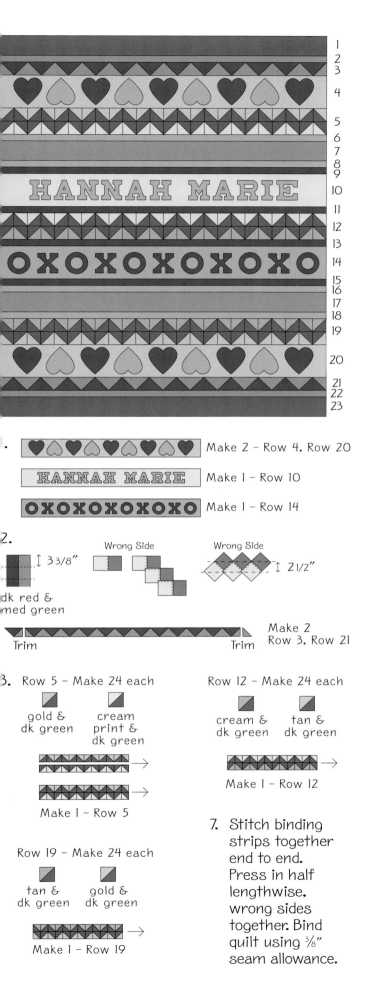

HANNAH MARIE

OXOXOXOXOXOXO

Make 2 - Row 4, Row 20

HANNAH MARIE — Make 1 - Row 10

OXOXOXOXOXOXO — Make 1 - Row 14

2.

↕ 3 3/8"

Wrong Side

Wrong Side

↕ 2 1/2"

dk red &
med green

Trim   Trim

Make 2
Row 3, Row 21

3. Row 5 – Make 24 each

gold &
dk green

cream
print &
dk green

Make 1 – Row 5

Row 19 – Make 24 each

tan &
dk green

gold &
dk green

Make 1 – Row 19

Row 12 – Make 24 each

cream &
dk green

tan &
dk green

Make 1 – Row 12

7. Stitch binding
strips together
end to end.
Press in half
lengthwise,
wrong sides
together. Bind
quilt using 3/8"
seam allowance.

DIRECTIONS

Use 1/4" seam allowance unless otherwise noted.

1. Applique Rows:
   a. For background of Row 10, stitch 2 strips together end to end and cut into one 48 1/2" piece. Repeat for Row 14. For Rows 4 & 20, stitch 3 strips together end to end and cut into two 48 1/2" pieces.
   b. Applique hearts (Rows 4 & 20), name (Row 10), and Xs and Os (Row 14). Keep appliques out of seam allowance. Our favorite method of applique is fusible web, and our patterns are set up for it—reversed for tracing and no seam allowances added.

2. Rows 3 & 21:
   a. Make 3 strip sets using cutting chart and diagram as guides. Press.
   b. Crosscut into 3 3/8" segments.
   c. Stitch 13 segments together, offsetting each one by placing raw edge 1/4" from seamline of previous segment (seams of each segment match). Press. Make 2.
   d. Trim points off edges of each strip, 1/4" outside seam intersections. Borders should be 2 1/2" wide. Trim ends 1/4" outside seam intersection as shown.

3. Rows 5, 12, 19:
   a. For Row 5, make 48 half-square triangle units using cutting chart and diagram as guides. Stitch row of gold/dark green units, rotating as shown. Stitch row of cream print/dark green units, rotating as shown. Stitch rows together.
   b. Make Row 12 with cream/dark green and tan/dark green units.
   c. Make Row 19 with tan/dark green and gold/dark green units.

4. Plain-fabric rows:
   a. Rows 1 & 23, Rows 2 & 22, Rows 7 & 17: Stitch 3 strips together end to end and cut into two 48 1/2" pieces.
   b. Rows 6, 8, 16, 18 & Rows 9, 11, 13, 15: Stitch 5 strips together end to end and cut into four 48 1/2" pieces.

5. Stitch all rows together. Press.

6. Piece backing horizontally to same size as batting. Layer and quilt as desired. Trim backing and batting even with top.

53

Woven Hearts

Photo on page 56

Approximate size 53 x 63" — 10" block

Use 42-45"-wide fabric. When strips appear in the cutting list, cut crossgrain strips (selvage to selvage).

YARDAGE

Blocks	⅜ yd each of 12 purples & blues
	¼ yd black for centers
Hearts	½ yd light purple
Border 1 &	
corner triangles	⅓ yd yellow
Border 2	1 yd dark purple
Border 3	½ yd medium purple
Binding	⅝ yd medium purple
Backing	3½ yd
Batting	59 x 69"

CUTTING

Blocks

Strip Set A	4 strips 2" wide of fabric 1
	4 strips 1" wide of fabric 2
	4 strips 2½" wide of fabric 3
Strip Set B	4 strips 2¼" wide of fabric 4
	4 strips 1¼" wide of fabric 5
	4 strips 2" wide of fabric 6
Strip Set C	4 strips 1½" wide of fabric 7
	4 strips 2" wide of fabric 8
	4 strips 2" wide of fabric 9
Strip Set D	4 strips 2½" wide of fabric 10
	4 strips 1½" wide of fabric 11
	4 strips 1½" wide of fabric 12
Centers	20 squares 2½" of black
Corner triangles	7 squares 1¾" of yellow
Hearts	12 – Pattern on page 37
Border 1	5 strips 1¼" wide
Border 2	6 strips 5" wide
Border 3	6 strips 2" wide
Binding	6-7 strips 2½" wide

We think this pattern would make a great quilt for a man or boy—just leave off the hearts. The block actually looks more complex than it is. It uses four different strip sets with strips of various widths and an easy partial-seam technique.

DIRECTIONS

Use ¼" seam allowance unless otherwise noted.

1. Make Strip Sets A-D using cutting chart and diagrams as guides. Press. Crosscut into 6½" segments.

2. Make 7 block centers with corner triangles by placing 1¾" square on 2½" square, right sides together, and stitching across small square diagonally. See diagram. Trim to ¼" seam allowance if desired. Press triangle to right side.

3. Make 20 blocks, each with one segment from each Strip Set. For the 7 blocks with corner triangles on the center square, vary the rotation of the center to get the triangles in different positions. (All blocks must be placed in quilt in same orientation.) See diagram.

4. Stitch blocks into 5 rows of 4. Stitch rows together. Press.

5. Applique hearts at block intersections as shown in whole quilt diagram.

6. Border 1: Measure length of quilt. Piece border strips to the measured length and stitch to sides of quilt. Repeat at top and bottom. Press.

7. Borders 2-3: Repeat Step 6.

8. Piece backing horizontally to same size as batting. Layer and quilt as desired. Trim backing and batting even with top.

9. Stitch binding strips together end to end. Press in half lengthwise, wrong sides together. Bind quilt using ⅜" seam allowance.

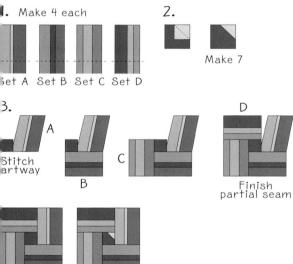

1. Make 4 each

Set A Set B Set C Set D

2.

Make 7

3.

A

B

C

D

Stitch partway

Finish partial seam

Make 13   Make 7

4.

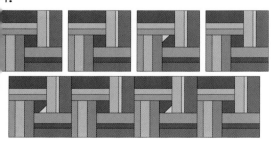

Sealed With a Kiss – Page 30

Simply Hearts

How easy can one quilt be? Make 40 four-patch blocks and cut half of them into hearts for the applique. Since plaids are not always prevalent in the marketplace, make it a point to always look and buy—it won't be long before you're ready to go. The quilt could always be made in your own special combination of solids and florals.

Photo on page 25

Approximate size 52 x 62" — 10" block

Use 42-45"-wide fabric. When strips appear in the cutting list, cut crossgrain strips (selvage to selvage).

YARDAGE

Blocks	¼ yd each of 12 or more plaids (yellow, orange, red, fuchsia, with some blue, green, & purple)
	¼ yd each of 12 or more monotone fabrics (yellow, orange, red, fuchsia)
Border 1	⅓ yd fuchsia
Border 2	1⅛ yd yellow
Binding	⅝ yd
Backing	3½ yd
Batting	58 x 68"
Fusible web	2½ yd

CUTTING

Blocks	80 squares 5½" plaids
	80 squares 5½" monotone fabrics
Applique	See pattern on page 37 & Step 2
Border 1	5 strips 1½" wide
Border 2	6 strips 5½" wide
Binding	6 strips 2½" wide

DIRECTIONS

Use ¼" seam allowance unless otherwise noted.

1. Make 20 plaid four-patch blocks and 20 monotone four-patch blocks following diagram. Press. Divide plaid blocks into 2 stacks of 10 each. Repeat with monotone blocks. Ten of each will be backgrounds, and 10 of each will be cut into hearts for applique.

2. Applique: Our favorite method of applique is fusible web, and our patterns are set up for it with no seam allowances added. Trace 20 hearts to fusible web including gray horizontal line. Cut out centers of hearts, leaving a ⅜" margin of fusible web inside the marked line. This reduces thickness and stiffness behind the applique. Fuse web to wrong sides of 10 plaid and 10 monotone blocks, matching gray horizontal lines and points at top and bottom of heart to seams. Cut out hearts. Fuse plaid hearts to monotone blocks and monotone hearts to plaid blocks, matching horizontal and vertical seamlines. Stitch in place with machine zigzag or blanket stitch.

3. Stitch blocks into 5 rows of 4 blocks each, alternating blocks with plaid hearts and blocks with plaid backgrounds. See diagram.

4. Stitch rows together. Press.

5. Border 1: Measure length of quilt. Piece border strips to the measured length and stitch to sides of quilt. Repeat at top and bottom. Press.

6. Border 2: Repeat Step 5.

7. Piece backing horizontally to same size as batting. Layer and quilt as desired. Trim backing and batting even with top.

8. Stitch binding strips together end to end. Press in half lengthwise, wrong sides together. Bind quilt using ⅜" seam allowance.

1.

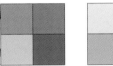

Make 20 –
Plaids

Make 20 –
Monotones

2.

Cut out 10 –
Plaids

Cut out 10 –
Monotones

Make 10 –
Plaid hearts
on monotone
backgrounds

Make 10 –
Monotone
hearts
on plaid
backgrounds

3.

Plaid
Heart

Plaid
Bkgrnd

Plaid
Heart

Plaid
Bkgrnd

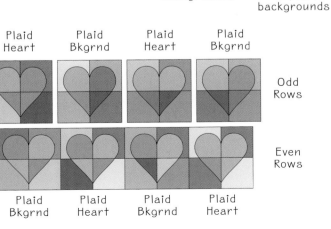

Odd
Rows

Even
Rows

Plaid
Bkgrnd

Plaid
Heart

Plaid
Bkgrnd

Plaid
Heart

Circle of Friends - Page 66

Country Hearts

Photo on page 64

Approximate size 42 x 54"

Use 42-45"-wide fabric. When strips appear in the cutting list, cut crossgrain strips (selvage to selvage).

YARDAGE

Blocks, Border 2

⅝ yd cream	⅜ yd pink #4	Borders 1, 3	¾ yd blue
¼ yd yellow #1	⅓ yd blue #1	Binding	⅝ yd
⅓ yd yellow #2	⅛ yd blue #2	Backing	2⅞ yd
½ yd yellow #3	1¼ yd blue #3	Batting	46 x 58"
¼ yd pink #1	⅝ yd green #1		
¼ yd pink #2	½ yd green #2		
¼ yd pink #3	¼ yd green #3		

CUTTING

*Cut these squares in HALF diagonally

Blocks, Border 2

cream	1 strip 2½" wide for Border 2
	1 rectangle 6½ x 12½" for Block 3
	1 rectangle 8½ x 10½" for Block 7
	8 squares 2½" for Blocks B & C
	*9 squares 2⅞" for Blocks B & C, filler strip
yellow #1	1 rectangle 8½ x 4½" for Block 9
	*2 squares 2⅞" for Block A
yellow #2	1 rectangle 12½ x 6½" for Block 1
	1 rectangle 6½ x 10½" for Block 11
	*2 squares 2⅞" for Block B
yellow #3	2 strips 2½" wide for Border 2
	1 rectangle 1½ x 8½" for filler strip
	*7 squares 2⅞" for filler strip
pink #1	*7 squares 2⅞" for filler strip
pink #2	1 square 2½" for Block C
pink #3	1 rectangle 1½ x 12½" for filler strip
	1 rectangle 1½ x 10½" for filler strip
pink #4	2 strips 2½" wide for Border 2
	*7 squares 2⅞" for Block C & filler strip
blue #1	1 rectangle 10½ x 4½" for Block 6
	1 rectangle 8½ x 6½" for Block 8
	*3 squares 2⅞" for Block A
	2 squares 2½" for Block B
blue #2	2 squares 2½" for Block B
	1 rectangle 1½ x 12½" for filler strip

Cutting continued on page 65.

DIRECTIONS

Use ¼" seam allowance unless otherwise noted.

1. Make 2 Block 4, 1 Block A, 1 Block B, and 1 Block C. See diagrams. Press.

2. Our favorite method of applique is fusible web, and our patterns are set up for it—reversed for tracing and no seam allowances added. Use leftover fabrics from making blocks. Applique blocks 1-12 and corner squares, keeping appliques out of seam allowances.

3. Make half-square triangle units for filler strips as shown. Press.

4. Lay out blocks on floor. Eight-inch filler strips go under Block B, 10" filler strips go under Block 5, and 12" filler strips go under Block 1. Pink/yellow filler triangle units go around Block 2, and pink/cream filler triangle units go to right of Blocks A and 3. Stitch into units as shown. Stitch units together. Press.

5. Border 1: Measure length of quilt. Cut border strips to the measured length and stitch to sides of quilt. Repeat at top and bottom. Press.

6. Border 2: Make strip sets as shown. Crosscut into 2½" segments. Make 2 side and 2 top/bottom borders. See diagram. Stitch side borders to quilt, adjusting seams to fit, if necessary. Stitch corner squares to top and bottom borders. Stitch to quilt, adjusting seams to fit, if necessary.

7. Border 3: Repeat Step 5, piecing border strips as needed.

8. Piece backing horizontally to same size as batting. Layer and quilt as desired. Trim backing and batting even with top.

9. Stitch binding strips together end to end. Press in half lengthwise, wrong sides together. Bind quilt using ⅜" seam allowance.

Block Names

1	A	4
2	3	4
5	6	B
	7	
8	C	11	12
9	10		

3.

Make 14
Block 2
Yellow #3 &
Pink #1

Make 9
Blocks A & 3
Cream &
Pink #4

4.

1	A	4
2	3	4
5	6	B
	7	
8	C	11	12
9	10		

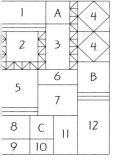

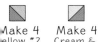

Make 3
Yellow #1 &
Blue #1

Make 2
Block 4
Blue #3 &
Green #1

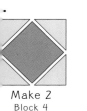

Block A

Make 4
Yellow #2
& Blue #3

Make 4
Cream &
Blue #3

Make 4
Cream &
Pink #4

Block B

Block C

Diagrams continued on page 65.

Diagrams continued on page 65.

63

COUNTRY HEARTS

Continued from page 62.

blue #3   7 strips 2½" wide for Border 2
*1 square 6⅞" for Block A
1 square 6¼" for Block 4
*2 squares 4⅞" for Block 4
*4 squares 2⅞" for Block B
1 rectangle 1½x10½" for filler strip
1 rectangle 6½x4½" for Block 10

green #1   1 square 10½x10½" for Block 5
1 square 6¼" for Block 4
*2 squares 4⅞" for Block 4
1 rectangle 8½x14½" for Block 12
4 squares 4½" for corners of
   Border 2

green #2   2 strips 2½" wide for Border 2
1 square 8½x8½" for Block 2

green #3   1 rectangle 1½x8½" for filler strip

Appliques   See patterns on pages 95-100
   & Step 2

Border 1   4 strips 1½" wide

Border 3   5 strips 2½" wide

Binding   5-6 strips 2½" wide

6.

Set 1	Set 2	Set 3	Set 4
Make 2	Make 2	Make 2	Make 1
Pink 4	Blue 3	Yellow 3	Blue 3
Blue 3	Green 2	Blue 3	Cream

Top & Bottom   Make 2

1 2 3 4 1 2 3 4 1 2 3 4 1 2 3

Inner Edge

Sides   Make 2

1 2 3 4 1 2 3 4 1 2 3 4 1 2 3 4 1 2 3 4 1

Inner Edge

Quilt Label

1. Cut piece of fabric slightly larger than label and iron freezer paper to wrong side. Make copy of label.
2. Trace label from copy with permanent pen using window or light box.
3. Use colored permanent marking pens to color as desired.
4. Remove paper. Cut out on gray line. Turn under ¼" and slipstitch to quilt.

For:

From my heart to your home,
this quilt was stitched with love for you!

By:

Date:

Circle of Friends

A quilt that would make a great gift for a friend, this design adapts well to a smaller version, or to making pillows. The coloration can be altered to match any decor. It would also make a good project for a small quilting club.

Photo on page 60

Approximate size 51 x 51" — 12" block

Use 42-45"-wide fabric. When strips appear in the cutting list, cut crossgrain strips (selvage to selvage).

YARDAGE

Blocks	1⅝ yd black for background
	⅓ yd blue
	⅙ yd each light gold, dark gold, & cream
	⅜ yd red
	⅝ yd green
Sashing rectangles	⅝ yd blue
Sashing squares	⅛ yd red
Border 1	¼ yd dark gold
Border 2	⅔ yd black
Border 3	½ yd red
Binding	⅝ yd
Backing	3½ yd
Batting	57 x 57"

CUTTING See Step 2 for applique details

Blocks
black	4 squares 12½" for wreaths
	5 rectangles 6½ x 12½" for baskets
	5 Pattern A, 5 Pattern A reversed – page 84
blue	*25 squares 3" for baskets
	4 squares 3½" for corner squares
light gold	*8 squares 3" for baskets
	16 berries for wreaths
dark gold	*3 squares 3" for baskets
cream	*5 squares 3" for baskets
red	5 squares 2⅝" for baskets
	35 hearts – page 84
green	15 triangles Pattern B for baskets – page 84
	5 stems ¼ x 3" for baskets
	30 leaves for baskets – page 84
	16 stem segments for wreaths - page 84
	96 leaves for wreaths – page 84
	8 leaves for corner squares – page 84
Sashing rectangles	24 rectangles 2 x 12½"
Sashing squares	16 squares 2"
Border 1	5 strips ⅞" wide
Border 2	5 strips 3½" wide
Border 3	6 strips 2" wide
Binding	6 strips 2½" wide

*Cut these squares in HALF diagonally

DIRECTIONS

Use ¼" seam allowance unless otherwise noted.

1. Make 5 basket blocks following diagram. Lower background pieces must be "set in" (stitched only to seam intersection). Applique heart flowers to top of each block. Our favorite method of applique is fusible web, and our patterns are set up for it—no seam allowances added. Press.

2. Using the quarter-wreath pattern on page 84 for layout, applique 4 wreath blocks. Press. Applique 4 corner squares for Border 2, keeping applique out of seam allowance.

3. Make 4 rows of sashing squares and rectangles. Make 2 rows of 2 baskets, 1 wreath, and 4 sashing rectangles. Make 1 row of 1 basket, 2 wreaths, and 4 sashing rectangles. See diagram.

4. Stitch alternating rows of blocks and sashing together. Press.

5. Border 1: Measure length of quilt. Piece border strips to the measured length and stitch to sides of quilt. Repeat at top and bottom. Press.

6. Border 2: Measure width and length of quilt. Piece border strips to the measured length and stitch to sides of quilt. Piece border strips to the measured width for top and bottom borders. Stitch applique squares to ends of top and bottom borders and stitch to quilt. Press.

7. Border 3: Repeat Step 5.

8. Piece backing to same size as batting. Layer and quilt as desired. Trim backing and batting even with top.

9. Stitch binding strips together end to end. Press in half lengthwise, wrong sides together. Bind quilt using ⅜" seam allowance.

Make 5
dark
gold &
light
gold

Make 10
light
gold &
blue

Make 10
cream
& blue

Make 5

2.

Make 4

Make 4

3.

Make 4

Make 2

Make 1

Crazy for You

Photo on page 64

Approximate size 41 x 51" — 9" block

Use 42-45"-wide fabric. When strips appear in the cutting list, cut crossgrain strips (selvage to selvage).

YARDAGE

Blocks & Border 2	⅙ yd each of 25 or more pastel prints
Sashing rectangles	½ yd blue
Sashing squares	⅛ yd lavender
Borders 1 & 3	¾ yd green
Border 2 & corner squares	½ yd yellow
Binding	½ yd green
Backing	2¾ yd
Batting	45 x 55"
Foundations	1 yd muslin or 12 pieces of paper larger than 9½" square

CUTTING

Sashing rectangles	31 rectangles 1½ x 9½"
Sashing squares	20 squares 1½"
Border 1	4 strips 1½" wide
Border 2 – pastels	6 strips 1½" wide – choose 6 of the darker fabrics – See Step 1
Border 2 – yellow	6 strips 1½" wide
Corner squares – yellow	4 squares 3½"
Corner squares – pastels	4 hearts – Pattern on page 37
Border 3	5 strips 2½" wide
Binding	5 strips 2½" wide
Foundations	12 squares 9½"

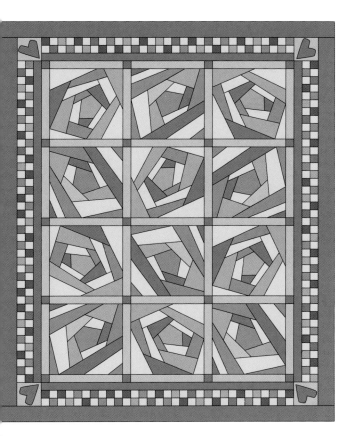

3.

5c. Border 2

Make 6

Make 2 – Top & Bottom

Make 2 – Sides

DIRECTIONS

Use ¼" seam allowance unless otherwise noted.

1. Cut Border 2 strips from 6 of the darker pastels and 4 hearts from desired fabrics. Set aside.

2. Make 12 crazy blocks using directions on page 73. Press.

3. Make 5 rows of sashing rectangles and sashing squares as shown. Make 4 rows of blocks and sashing rectangles as shown.

4. Stitch rows of sashing and rows of blocks together. Press.

5. Border 1-2:

   a. Measure length and width of quilt. Cut Border 1 strips to the measured length for sides. Cut Border 1 strips to the measured length for top and bottom. Set aside.

   b. Applique hearts to corner squares, keeping heart out of seam allowance. Set aside. Our favorite method of applique is fusible web, and our patterns are set up for it—reversed for tracing and no seam allowances added.

   c. Make 6 strip sets, each with one 1½" yellow strip and one 1½" strip from Step 1. Crosscut into 1½" segments. Stitch into 2 borders of 31 segments and 2 borders of 41 segments as shown.

   d. For each side of quilt, stitch Border 1 strip to Border 2. Adjust seams in Border 2 to fit Border 1, if necessary.

   e. Stitch Border 1-2 units to sides of quilt. Stitch corner squares to each end of top and bottom border units. Stitch Border 1-2 units to top and bottom. Press.

6. Border 3: Measure length of quilt. Cut border strips to the measured length and stitch to sides of quilt. Repeat at top and bottom. Press.

7. Piece backing horizontally to same size as batting. Layer and quilt as desired. Trim backing and batting even with top.

8. Stitch binding strips together end to end. Press in half lengthwise, wrong sides together. Bind quilt using ⅜" seam allowance.

Heartbeats

One of the best ways to make the one-inch half-square triangle units for Border 3 in this quilt is with paper piecing. Check with your local quilt shop or online for Thangles™ or Triangles on a Roll. They work great. Note: Extra yardage may be needed for paper piecing.

Photo on page 28

Approximate size 43 x 51" — 8" block

Use 42-45"-wide fabric. When strips appear in the cutting list, cut crossgrain strips (selvage to selvage).

YARDAGE

Blocks, appliques, & Border 2	⅜ yd each of 9 or more yellows, blues, & greens
Border 1 & corners of Border 2-3	⅛ yd each of 5 or more creams
Border 3	⅓ yd each of blue & cream
Border 4	½ yd blue
Binding	½ yd yellow
Backing	2⅞ yd
Batting	47 x 55"

CUTTING

Blocks	20 squares 8½"
Applique	See pattern on page 43 & Step 2
Border 1	36 rectangles 2½ x 4½"
	4 squares 2½"
Border 2	36 rectangles 1½ x 4½"
Border 3	*72 squares 1⅞" – blue
	*72 squares 1⅞" – cream
	OR 144 half-square triangle units that finish at 1"
Border 2-3 Corners	24 squares 1½" – blue & green
	24 squares 1½" – cream
Border 4	5 strips 2" wide
Binding	5 strips 2½" wide

*Cut these squares in HALF diagonally

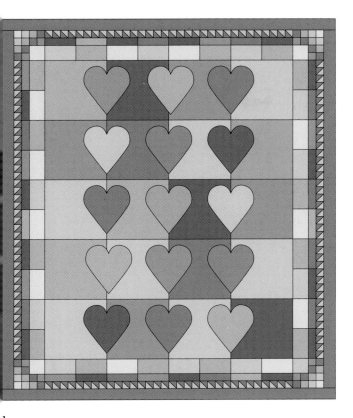

1.

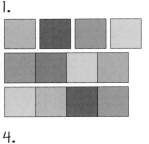

4.

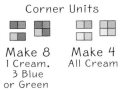

Make 144
Cream
& Blue

Make 36

Corner Units

Make 8
1 Cream,
3 Blue
or Green

Make 4
All Cream

Side Borders – Make 2   C = Cream

Top/Bottom Borders – Make 2

DIRECTIONS

Use ¼″ seam allowance unless otherwise noted.

1. Stitch 8½″ squares into 5 rows of 4. Stitch rows together. Press.

2. Applique hearts to seams between squares as shown. Our favorite method of applique is fusible web, and our patterns are set up for it with no seam allowances added.

3. Border 1: Piece 2 side borders using 10 rectangles each. Stitch to quilt. Piece top/bottom borders using 8 rectangles each. Stitch squares to each end. Stitch to quilt. Press.

4. Border 2-3:
   a. Make 36 units with one 1½ x 4½″ rectangle and four half-square triangle units, as shown. Press.
   b. Make 8 dark corner units with 1½″ squares as shown. Make 4 light corner units with 1½″ squares as shown. Press.
   c. Piece 2 side borders using 10 rectangular units and 2 dark corner units each. Rotate corner units as shown. Stitch to quilt. Piece top/bottom borders using 8 rectangular units and 2 dark corner units each. Stitch light corner units to each end, rotated as shown. Stitch to quilt. Press.

5. Border 4: Measure length of quilt. Piece border strips to the measured length and stitch to sides of quilt. Repeat at top and bottom. Press.

6. Piece backing horizontally to same size as batting. Layer and quilt as desired. Trim backing and batting even with top.

7. Stitch binding strips together end to end. Press in half lengthwise, wrong sides together. Bind quilt using ⅜″ seam allowance.

HEARTBEATS WALL HANGING

Photo on page 28

Approximate size 43 x 19" — 8" block

Use 42-45"-wide fabric. When strips appear in the cutting list, cut crossgrain strips (selvage to selvage).

YARDAGE

Blocks, appliques, & Border 2 — ¼ yd each of 8 yellows, blues, & greens

Stars & Border 1 — ⅓ yd each of 4 creams
Border 3 — ¼ yd each of blue & cream
Border 4 — ⅜ yd blue
Binding — ⅜ yd yellow
Backing — 1½ yd
Batting — 47 x 23"

CUTTING

Blocks – for 1
- 1 square 4½" – cream
- *4 squares 2⅞" – cream
- 4 squares 2½" – blue, green, or yellow
- *4 squares 2⅞" – blue, green, or yellow

Applique
- 4 – See pattern on page 43 & Step 3

Border 1
- 20 rectangles 2½ x 4½"
- 4 squares 2½"

Border 2
- 20 rectangles 1½ x 4½"

Border 3
- *40 squares 1⅞" – blue
- *40 squares 1⅞" – cream
- OR 80 half-square triangle units that finish at 1"

Border 2-3 corners
- 24 squares 1½" – blue & green
- 24 squares 1½" – cream

Border 4
- 4 strips 2" wide

Binding
- 4 strips 2½" wide

*Cut these squares in HALF diagonally

DIRECTIONS

Use ¼" seam allowance unless otherwise noted.

1. Make 4 star blocks following diagram. Press.
2. Stitch blocks into 1 row of 4. Press.
3. Applique hearts to blocks. Our favorite method of applique is fusible web, and our patterns are set up for it with no seam allowances added.

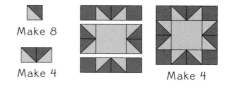

1. For each block

Make 8

Make 4

Make 4

4. Border 1: Piece 2 side borders using 2 rectangles each. Stitch to wall hanging. Piece top/bottom borders using 8 rectangles each. Stitch squares to each end. Stitch to wall hanging. Press.

5. Border 2-3:
   a. Make 20 units with one 1½ x 4½" rectangle and four half-square triangle units, as shown in diagram on page 71. Press.
   b. Make 8 dark corner units with 1½" squares as shown. Make 4 light corner units with 1½" squares as shown. Press.
   c. Piece 2 side borders using 2 rectangular units and 2 dark corner units each. Rotate corner units as shown. Stitch to quilt. Piece top/bottom borders using 8 rectangular units and 2 dark corner units each. Stitch light corner units to each end, rotated as shown. Stitch to quilt.

6. Border 4: Measure length of quilt. Cut border strips to the measured length and stitch to sides of wall hanging. Repeat at top and bottom, piecing strips end to end if necessary. Press.

7. Layer and quilt as desired. Trim backing and batting even with top.

8. Stitch binding strips together end to end. Press in half lengthwise, wrong sides together. Bind quilt using ⅜" seam allowance.

Quilt Label

See directions for use on page 65.

CRAZY QUILT BLOCKS - 9"

Use ¼" seam allowance unless otherwise noted.

1. For each block, cut out one 9½" square of paper or muslin for foundation.

2. Cut strips of fabrics for blocks 1½" to 3" wide.

3. For center, cut a three- to five-sided piece of fabric approximately 4-5" in diameter.

4. Place center piece on muslin/paper square, somewhere near the middle of the square, right side up.

5. Lay strip on center piece, right sides together, raw edges even. Stitch. Fold strip over and trim end.

6. Continue adding strips clockwise or counterclockwise. To get a variety of shapes, lay strips on at different angles. Trim away excess at seam allowances as you go to prevent block from getting too bulky.

7. Trim overhanging strips to edge of muslin/paper square. Tear away paper if used.

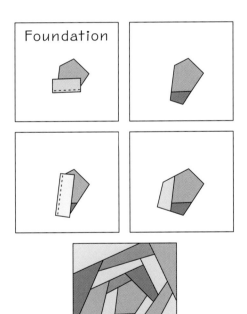

Home is Where the Heart is

Use some of the blocks from Home Is Where the Heart Is to make pillows for chairs in the room where the quilt is displayed. The quilt could be personalized by stitching family names and addresses in the borders.

Photo on page 52

Approximate size 49 x 40"

Use 42-45"-wide fabric. When strips appear in the cutting list, cut crossgrain strips (selvage to selvage).

YARDAGE

Block backgrounds	
sky & grass	⅓ yd each of 4-6 yellows
	⅓ yd each of 5-7 blues & greens
Blocks & appliques	⅓ yd each of 8-10 bright plaids
	⅙ yd each of 10-12 bright prints – pink, purple, red, yellow, orange, green, light green, blue, light blue
	¼ yd dark green for big tree
	⅛ yd light blue for lettering
Border 1	¼ yd yellow
Border 2	⅓ yd bright green
Border 3	¼ yd bright blue
	¼ yd red plaid
Border 4	⅝ yd medium blue
	⅙ yd red plaid
Binding	¾ yd red plaid
Backing	2¾ yd
Batting	53 x 44"
Fusible web	2 yd

CUTTING

Backgrounds	
House block A	1 rectangle 9½ x 8½"
	1 rectangle 9½ x 1½"
House block B	1 rectangle 9½ x 7¼"
	1 rectangle 9½ x 1¼"
	1 rectangle 9½ x 2"
House block C	1 rectangle 9½ x 7"
	1 rectangle 9½ x 3"
House block D	1 rectangle 8½ x 12½"
	1 rectangle 8½ x 3½"
House blocks E	2 rectangles 6½ x 5¾"
	2 rectangles 6½ x ¾"
	2 rectangles 6½ x 1"
Small tree blocks	5 squares 3½" – light blue, green
Pine tree block	1 rectangle 6½ x 17"
	4 squares 2"
Heart tree block	1 rectangle 4½ x 15½"
Heart flower block (1 flower)	1 rectangle 6½ x 9½"
Heart flower block (3 flowers)	1 rectangle 9½ x 6½"

Cutting continued on page 76.

HOME IS WHERE THE HEART IS

DIRECTIONS

Use ¼" seam allowance unless otherwise noted.

1. Make Log Cabin, four-patch, and patchwork heart blocks as shown. Press.

2. Applique

   a. Piece backgrounds for all applique blocks, including heart checkerboard (shown). Lay out all blocks on floor. Stitch into 6 large units as shown.

   b. Applique houses, trees, flowers, and heart checkerboard unit, keeping applique out of seam allowance. Hearts on tops of small tree blocks overlap nearby blocks and borders and can be added now or after quilt top is finished depending on their location in the quilt. Our favorite method of applique is fusible web, and our patterns are set up for it—reversed for tracing and no seam allowances added.

3. Stitch units into 3 vertical panels, then stitch panels together. Press.

4. Border 1: Measure length of quilt. Cut border strips to the measured length and stitch to sides of quilt. Repeat at top and bottom. Press.

5. Border 2: Repeat Step 4.

6. Border 3: Stitch 2" squares into 2 border units of 21 squares each for sides of quilt. Stitch squares into 2 border units of 29 squares each for top and bottom of quilt. Press. Adjust to fit quilt if necessary. Stitch side borders to quilt, then top and bottom borders.

7. Border 4: Measure width and length of quilt. Cut border strips to the measured length and stitch to sides of quilt. Cut border strips to the measured width for top and bottom borders. Applique bottom Border 4, keeping applique out of seam allowance. Stitch corner squares to ends of each. Stitch borders to quilt. Press.

8. Piece backing vertically to same size as batting. Layer and quilt as desired. Trim backing and batting even with top.

9. Stitch binding strips together end to end. Press in half lengthwise, wrong sides together. Bind quilt using ⅜" seam allowance.

1.

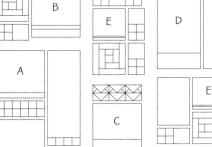

Make 6   Make 3

Make 3 Make 3   Make 3 Make 3   Make 3

2.

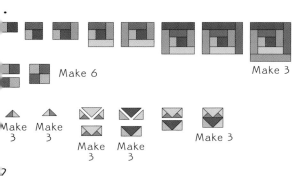

Heart Checkerboard
Background – Make 1

3.

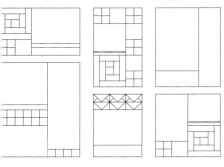

HOME IS WHERE THE HEART IS

Continued from page 74.

Log Cabin blocks	3 squares 2″ for centers
	assorted strips 1⅝″ for logs
Four-patch blocks	12 squares 2″ – green
	12 squares 2″ – orange
Patchwork heart blocks	**1 square 4¼″ – purple
	**2 squares 2¾″ – bright pink
	**1 square 4¼″ – orange
	**2 squares 2¾″ – orange
	*3 squares 2⅜″ – orange
Heart checkerboard	6 squares 2″ – bright blue
	6 squares 2″ – medium blue
Appliques	See patterns on pages 85-90 & Step 2
Border 1	4 strips 1½″ wide
Border 2	4 strips 1¾″ wide
Border 3	50 squares 2″ – bright blue
	50 squares 2″ – red plaid
Border 4	4 strips 3½″ wide – medium blue
	4 squares 3½″ – red plaid
Binding	bias strips 2½″ wide to equal 200″

*Cut these squares in HALF diagonally
**Cut these squares in QUARTERS diagonally

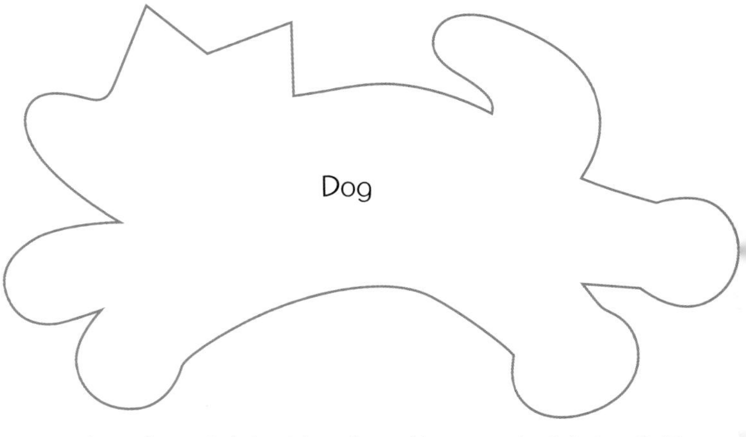

DOG PIN

Photo on page 52

MATERIALS

Dog body	⅛ yd or scrap
Freezer paper	scrap
Brass wire	12-16″ piece, 18- or 20-gauge
Silk ribbon	scrap
Gold cording	scrap
Sequins	
Seed beads	
Craft glue	
Wire cutters	
Stuffing	
Pin back	

CUTTING

Dog body   2 rectangles 3½ x 5″

DIRECTIONS

1. Trace dog pattern (above) to freezer paper and cut out. Press freezer paper, centered, to wrong side of one of the dog body fabric rectangles. Place dog body rectangles right sides together and stitch all the way around edge of freezer paper using a short stitch length. Remove freezer paper. Trim ⅛″ outside of stitching line.

2. Cut 1″ slit in back of dog body. Clip. Turn right side out. Stuff firmly. Stitch opening closed.

3. Wrap silk ribbon and gold cording around dog's middle. Wrap brass wire over ribbon and cording, leaving a 2-3″ ends. Wrap the wire ends around a pencil, creating spirals.

4. Thread beads and sequins on wire. Glue a bead to each end to keep loose beads from falling off.

5. Stitch beads and sequins to dog body for eye, nose, and "spots".

6. Stitch pin back to back of dog body.

Dog

CHENILLE RUG

Photo on page 24

Approximate size 35x29"

Use 42-45"-wide fabric.

Use fabrics with woven, not printed, design (i.e., both sides of the fabric are the same). We used solid and buffalo-checked flannel, but woven homespun would work also.

YARDAGE

Base/Layer 1	2¼ yd black solid
Layer 2/3	2¼ yd black/pink check – lge heart
Layer 4/5	1 yd red solid – med heart
Layer 6/7	⅝ yd orange solid – sm heart
Binding	½ yd black solid
Pattern paper	

DIRECTIONS

Use ¼" seam allowance unless otherwise noted.

1. Cut 40x36" rectangles: 2 black, 2 black/pink check. Layer, right side up, both black rectangles then both black/pink, keeping selvages (lengthwise grain of fabric) in same position in each layer. Press layers together well.

   Note: DO NOT CUT these rectangles into heart shape until after chenille is stitched, washed, and dried, Step 9 below.

2. Draw and cut out paper patterns for three sizes of hearts using grid at right.

3. Using patterns, cut 2 medium hearts from red solid and 2 small hearts from orange solid, keeping lengthwise grain running from top to bottom in each.

4. Lay large paper heart on layered rectangles, leaving a 3" margin all around. Mark around edge of paper pattern with chalk. Remove. Use chalk line as a guide to place both red and then both orange hearts on layered rectangles. Pinbaste sparsely.

5. Draw parallel lines at a 45° angle ⅜" apart across right side of entire layered piece (or mark only the first 45° line and then use the edge of an even-feed foot as a guide for stitching the remaining lines).

6. Add more pinbasting.

7. Starting across the center, machine stitch along all drawn lines with black thread, removing pins as you go.

2.

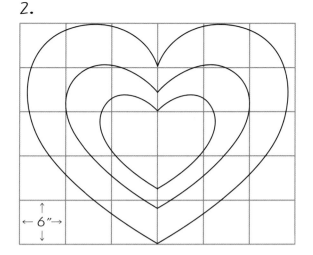

← 6" →

4.

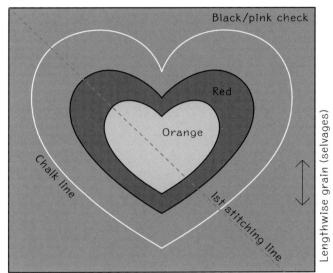

Black/pink check

Red

Orange

Chalk line

1st stitching line

Lengthwise grain (selvages)

8. Using scissors or a special chenille cutter, cut all layers EXCEPT BASE (bottom black layer) between the stitching lines.

9. Machine wash and dry rectangular chenille piece.

10. Pin large paper heart pattern to rectangle, making sure to center it over medium and small hearts. Draw line around pattern directly on chenille using a permanent marker. Remove pattern. Zigzag along line to stabilize. Cut out large heart shape just outside zigzag stitching.

11. Binding: Cut BIAS strips 2½" wide and stitch end to end to equal 120". Press in half lengthwise, wrong sides together. Bind rug using ⅜" seam allowance.

CONVERSATION HEARTS PICTURES

Photo on page 24

Makes three 12" square framed pictures

YARDAGE & MATERIALS

Base squares	½ yd each of 3 fabrics
Appliques	¼ yd each of 5-7 fabrics or scraps up to 12" square
	⅜ yd for largest heart or scrap 12" square
Fusible web	1 yd
Black metal frames	three 12" square frames – it works well to get the kind that come 2 sides in a package & get 6 packages
Matboard	3 squares 12" – black
Spray adhesive	

CUTTING

Base squares & appliques   Patterns on pages 101-103

DIRECTIONS

1. Applique heart designs to base squares. Our favorite method of applique is fusible web, and our patterns are set up for it—reversed for tracing and no seam allowances added.

2. Use spray adhesive to mount appliqued pieces on matboard.

3. Insert matboard pieces into frames.

PLATE CHARMERS

Photo on page 25

YARDAGE & MATERIALS for 1

2 round clear glass plates for 1 place setting
2 squares background fabric larger than plates
fabric scraps for applique
fusible web
paper pattern of base of plate

DIRECTIONS

1. Prepare fusible web applique pieces. Patterns on page 83 (reduce or enlarge on photocopier as needed). Center design on a square of background fabric 2-3" bigger than paper pattern. For grass on house Plate Charmer, fuse a rectangle of "grass" fabric to the bottom of the square of background fabric. Fuse house or heart design in place.

2. Backing: Bond a square of fusible web to wrong side of Plate Charmer. Peel paper and fuse to wrong side of other fabric square.

3. Using paper pattern, and centering design within circle, cut out Plate Charmer.

4. Place Plate Charmer between two plates.

PLATE MATS

Photo on page 25

12" circle

YARDAGE & MATERIALS for 1

1 round clear glass plate for 1 place setting
½ yd background fabric
fabric scraps for applique
⅓ yd fabric for bias binding
½ yd fusible web
14" square of batting

DIRECTIONS

1. Cut out two 12½" circles of background fabric and one of batting. Layer fabric circles wrong sides together with batting between them and press well. Baste outside edges together.

2. Prepare fusible web applique pieces. Patterns below. Center design on mat. Fuse in place. Machine applique if desired.

3. Cut enough bias strips to equal 45" when sewn end to end. Stitch strips together end to end. Bind mat with ⅜" seam allowance.

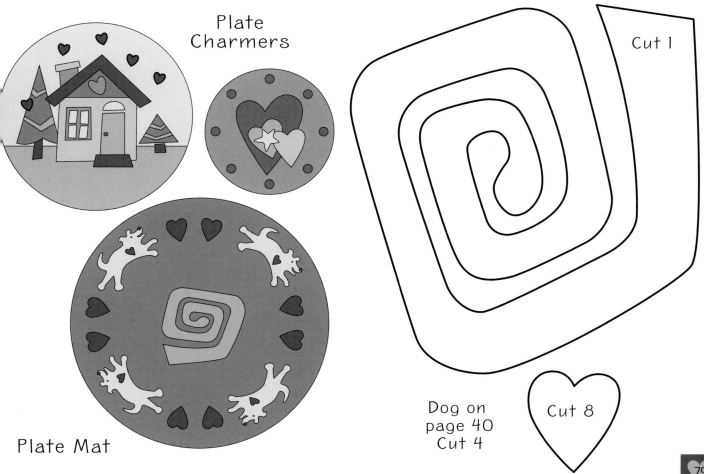

Plate Charmers

Plate Mat

Cut 1

Dog on page 40
Cut 4

Cut 8

79

APARTMENT ROW PIN

Photo on page 52

MATERIALS
Matboard scraps
Fabric scraps
Gold cording
Fine beading wire
Seed beads
Craft glue
Craft knife
Fusible web
Pin back

CUTTING

Matboard	3 houses – pattern below 1 rectangle ½ x 4"
Fabric backed with fusible web	3 houses, all pieces 1 rectangle ½ x 4"

DIRECTIONS

1. Fuse fabric pieces to matboard pieces. Use tiny dots of glue and/or a stiletto or awl to hold pieces in place (to avoid burning yourself).

2. Make 3 "smoke" strands: Thread 12-18 beads on 5-6" piece of wire. Thread wire back down through row of beads, skipping the end bead. See diagram. Leave 1½" tails of wire. Glue the wires of each smoke strand to the back of a chimney, ends extending down to the middle of the house. Fuse or glue a scrap of fabric over the wire to hold it in place.

3. Glue houses to rectangle, spacing evenly.

4. Wrap gold cording around bar, gluing ends on back. Glue beads to doors for doorknobs.

5. Glue pin back to back of row of houses.

2.

BEADED POUCH NECKLACE

Photo on page 21

MATERIALS

Front	⅛ yd or scrap
Back	⅛ yd or scrap
Lining	⅛ yd or scrap
Rat tail cording	1 yd
Large heart button	
Large snap	
Beaded trim on ribbon base (premade)	
Loose beads that match beaded trim	

DIRECTIONS

Use ¼" seam allowance unless otherwise noted.

1. Front: Cut 1 rectangle 3½ x 4" from front fabric and 1 from lining fabric. Place right sides together and stitch 2 long and 1 short side. Clip and turn. Press ¼" seam allowance to inside on open bottom edge.

2. Back: Cut 1 rectangle 3½ x 5½" from back fabric and 1 from lining fabric. Place right sides together. Trim one end of both rectangles into a point as shown. Stitch long sides and pointed end. Clip and turn. Press ¼" seam allowance to inside on open bottom edge.

3. Place front on back matching long sides and bottom edges. Sandwich ribbon of beaded trim between the front and back at the bottom edge. Pin and then topstitch side and bottom edges through all layers. A zipper foot helps get close to the beading along the bottom edge.

4. Handstitch loose beads over topstitching at sides and along edge on right side of flap.

5. Stitch button to front of pouch below flap. Handstitch cording under flap and knot ends together, adjusting necklace to desired length.

6. Stitch snap parts to front and flap for closing.

1 3/4"

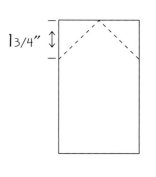

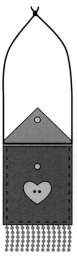

SHREDDED FABRIC NECKLACE

Photo on page 52

MATERIALS

Front/back	⅙ yd or scrap
Lining	⅙ yd or scrap
Rat tail cording	1¾ yd
Bright scraps of 100% cottons	
Soluble stabilizer	
Large heart button	
Large snap	
Optional: large bead	

DIRECTIONS

Use ¼" seam allowance unless otherwise noted.

1. Cut 1 rectangle 5x10¼" from front/back fabric and 1 the same size from lining fabric.

2. Place rectangles right sides together. Trim one end of both rectangles into a point as shown in diagram. Stitch around entire outside edge, leaving 2" open on short straight edge for turning. Clip, turn, press. Stitch opening closed.

3. Fold short straight side up toward pointed end 3½" to form pocket. Press.

4. Make shredded fabric
   a. Cut ⅛-¼" (wide) by 1½-2" (long) slivers of the bright fabrics.
   b. Cut 2 rectangles of soluble stabilizer 7x9".
   c. Sprinkle shredded fabric pieces ⅛-¼" deep on one piece of the soluble stabilizer. Cover with other piece of stabilizer. Pin layers together.
   d. Using transparent thread on machine, stitch around outside edge of rectangles. Use of a walking foot helps. Stitch over entire piece with straight or curvy lines about ¼" apart to hold shreds.
   e. Following manufacturer's directions, dissolve stabilizer in water. Dry flat.

5. Lay folded pocket on shredded fabric and trim shredded fabric ¼" larger than pocket. See diagram.

6. Topstitch through all layers along sides and bottom of pocket. See diagram.

7. Stitch snap parts to front and flap for closing. Stitch heart button to outside of flap over snap.

8. Hand stitch cording to sides and bottom of pocket. Run cording through shredded fabric at top. Tie knot in cording at top, adjusting length as desired, or glue ends into a large bead.

2.

↕ 2 1/4"

5.

Trim

Fold

6.

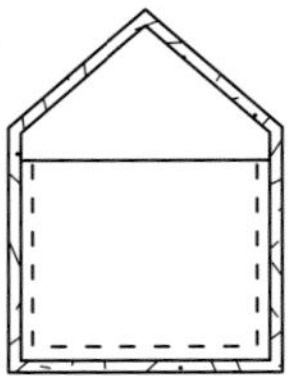

Topstitch

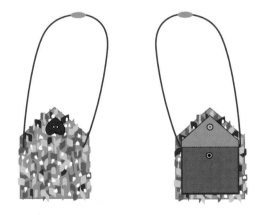

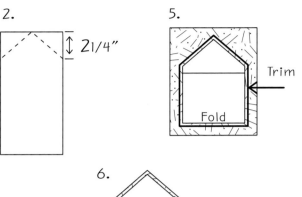

HEART PINS

Photos on pages 17, 21

MATERIALS

Corrugated cardboard or matboard scraps
Fabric scraps
Thin batting scraps
Fusible web
Craft glue
Craft knife
Pin backs
Embroidery floss
Polymer clay, ceramic, or other decorative buttons
Beaded trim on ribbon base (premade)

DIRECTIONS

1. Cut out desired shapes from cardboard and batting using dotted lines on patterns below.

2. Backgrounds: Trace squares, rectangles, and/or hearts to fusible web using dotted lines. Cut out leaving 1″ margin. Fuse to scraps of fabric. Cut out shapes ½″ outside dotted line.

3. Applique designs to backgrounds using fusible web. Mix and match elements from patterns as desired. Remove paper from backgrounds.

4. Optional: Add hand stitches and French knots with embroidery floss.

5. Glue batting to cardboard base. Place background over batting and center the design. Use light source from behind if needed. Wrap edges of background fabric to back of cardboard base, clipping and trimming where necessary, and fuse to back of cardboard.

6. Backing: Trace squares, rectangles, and/or hearts to fusible web using dotted lines. Fuse to desired backing fabric. Trim away ⅛″ or so around entire edge. Fuse to back of pin, covering raw edges from Step 5.

7. Optional: Glue buttons to pins.

8. Optional: Glue beaded trim to bottom edge of selected pins.

9. Glue a pin back to back of each pin.

HOUSE PIN & HEART EARRINGS

Photo on page 21

MATERIALS

Corrugated wave paper
Adhesive-backed glitter & foil papers
Craft knife
Craft glue
Pin back
Earring backs

DIRECTIONS

1. Cut out house and hearts from corrugated paper using dotted lines on patterns (page 83).

2. Cut out designs from adhesive-backed papers and apply to corrugated paper base.

3. Glue a pin back to back of pin and earring backs to backs of earrings.

House Pin & Heart Earrings

Cut 1

Cut 1

Cut 1

Cut 1

Cut 1

Cut 8

Plate Charmers

Cut 1

Cut 1

Cut 1

Cut 5

Circle of Friends

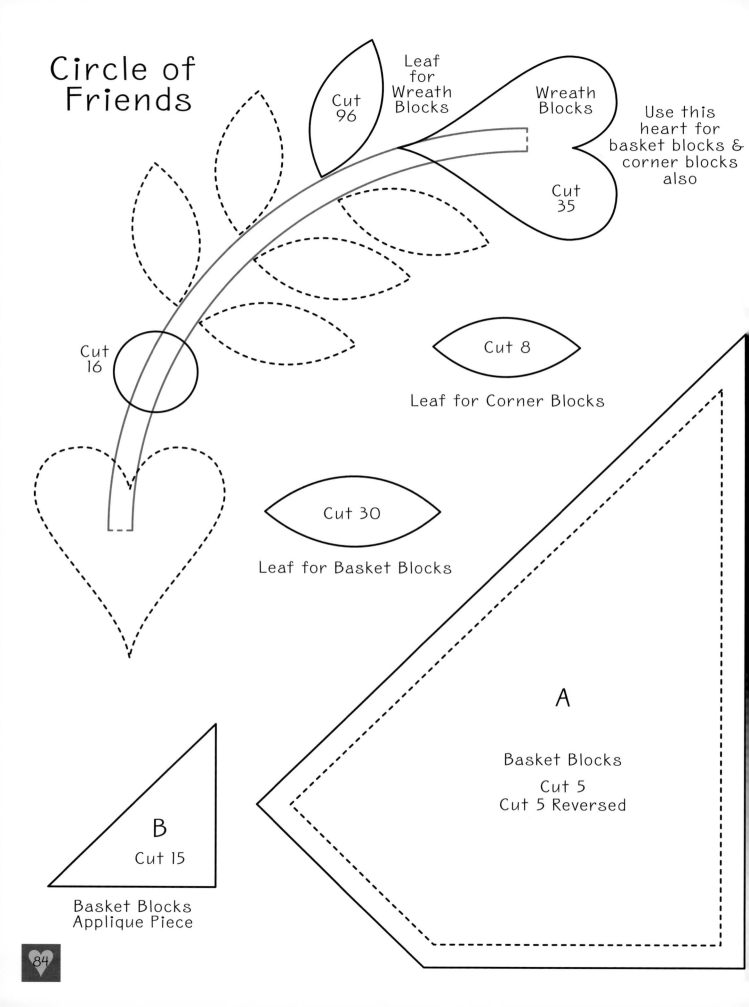

Leaf for Wreath Blocks
Cut 96

Wreath Blocks
Cut 35

Use this heart for basket blocks & corner blocks also

Cut 16

Cut 8

Leaf for Corner Blocks

Cut 30

Leaf for Basket Blocks

A

Basket Blocks

Cut 5
Cut 5 Reversed

B
Cut 15

Basket Blocks
Applique Piece

Match to dotted line at left for full pattern

Match to dotted line at right for full pattern

Cut 1

Cut 2

Three-flower Block

Three-flower Block

Cut 4

Cut 8

Cut 1

Cut 2

Cut 6 for Heart Checkerboard

Home Is Where the Heart Is

Patterns are reversed for tracing to fusible web

Tree Trunk

Pine Tree Block

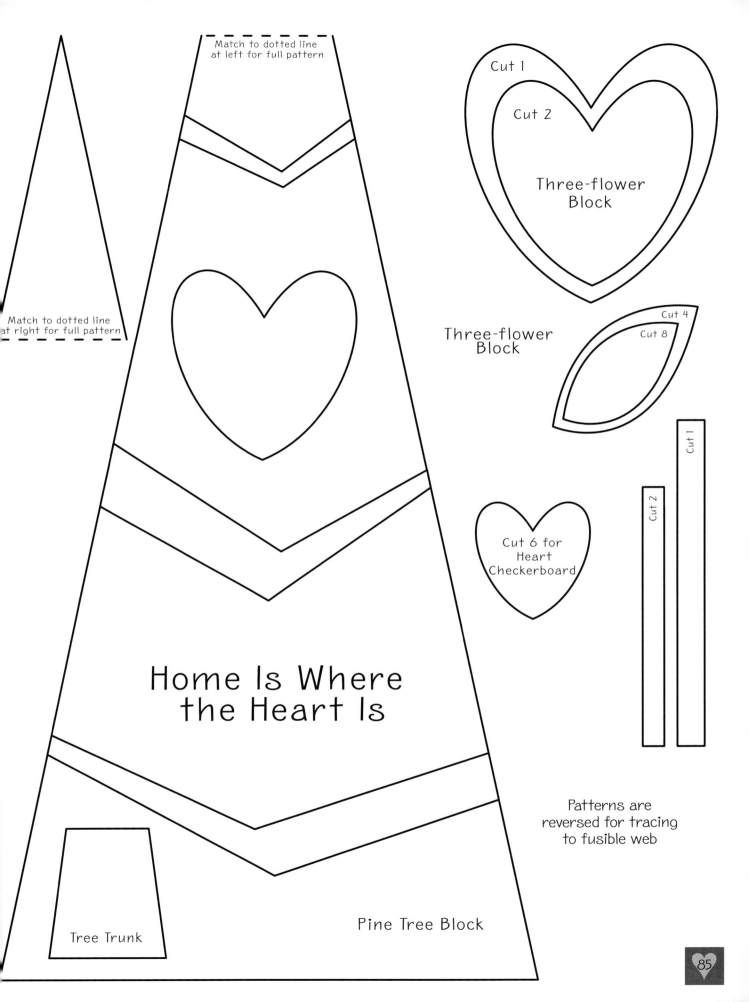

Home Is Where the Heart Is

HOME IS WHERE

Block E –
Cut 2
of each

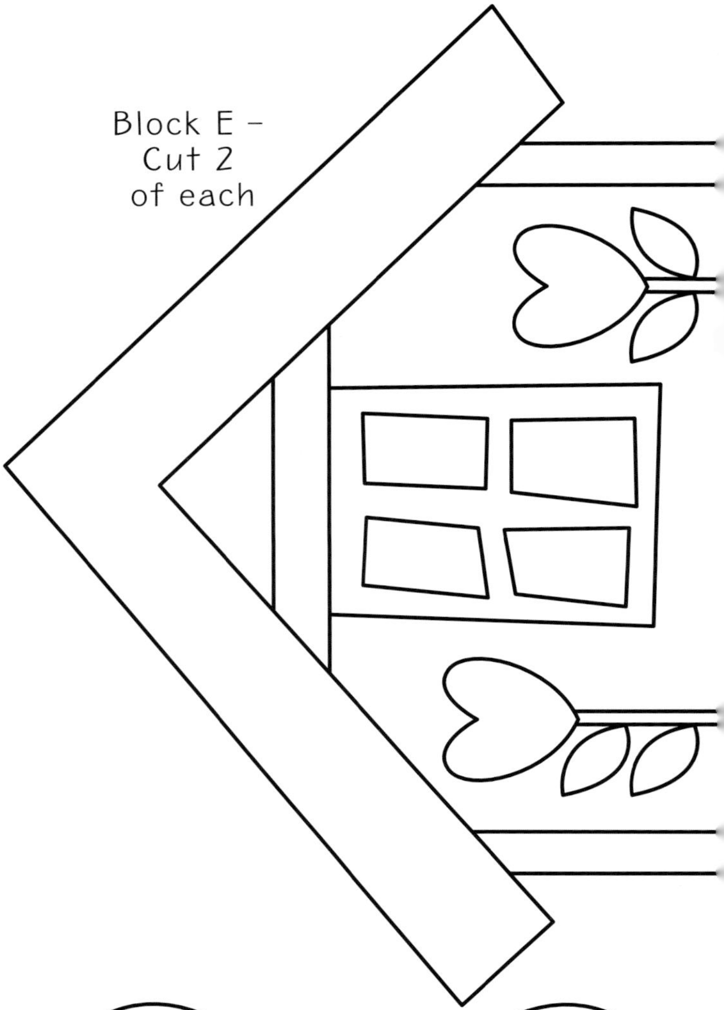

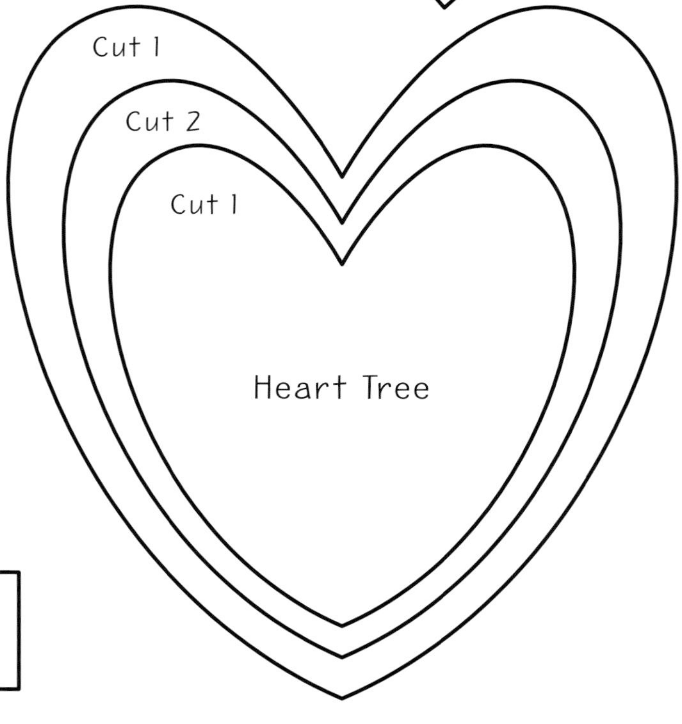

Patterns are reversed for tracing to fusible web

Tree Trunk   Cut 1

Cut 1

Cut 2

Cut 1

Heart Tree

Home Is Where
the Heart Is

Small
Tree
Blocks

Block C

Patterns are reversed for tracing to fusible web

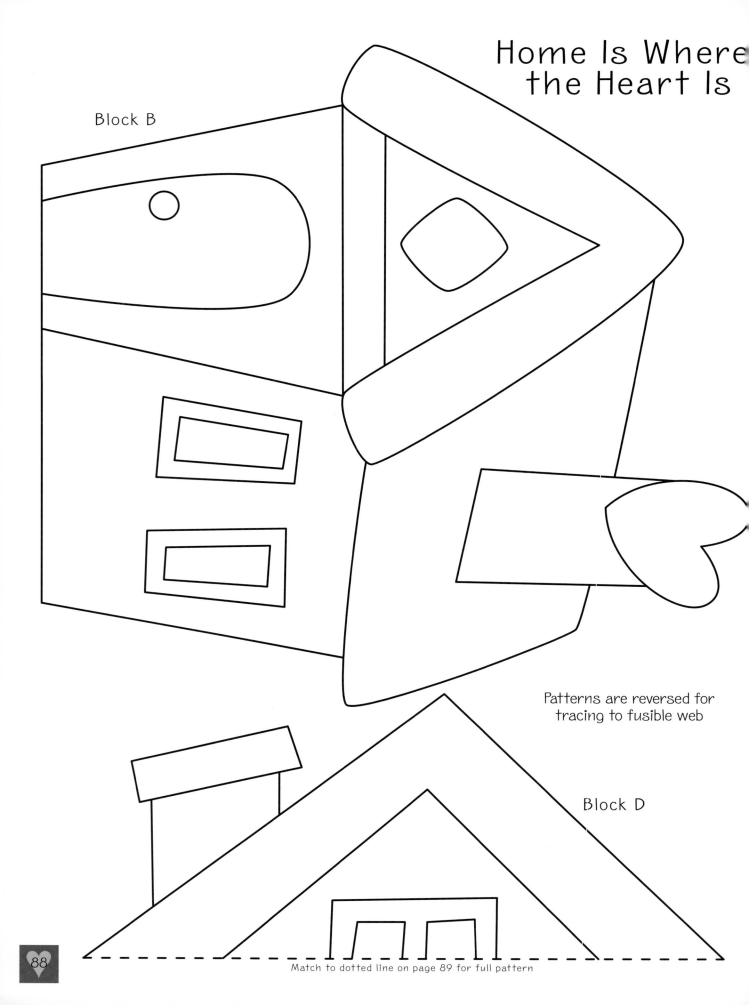

Home Is Where
the Heart Is

Block B

Patterns are reversed for
tracing to fusible web

Block D

88

Match to dotted line on page 89 for full pattern

Match to dotted line on page 88 for full pattern

Block D

Home
Is
Where
the
Heart
Is

Patterns are reversed for tracing to fusible web

Match to dotted line on page 88 for full pattern

89

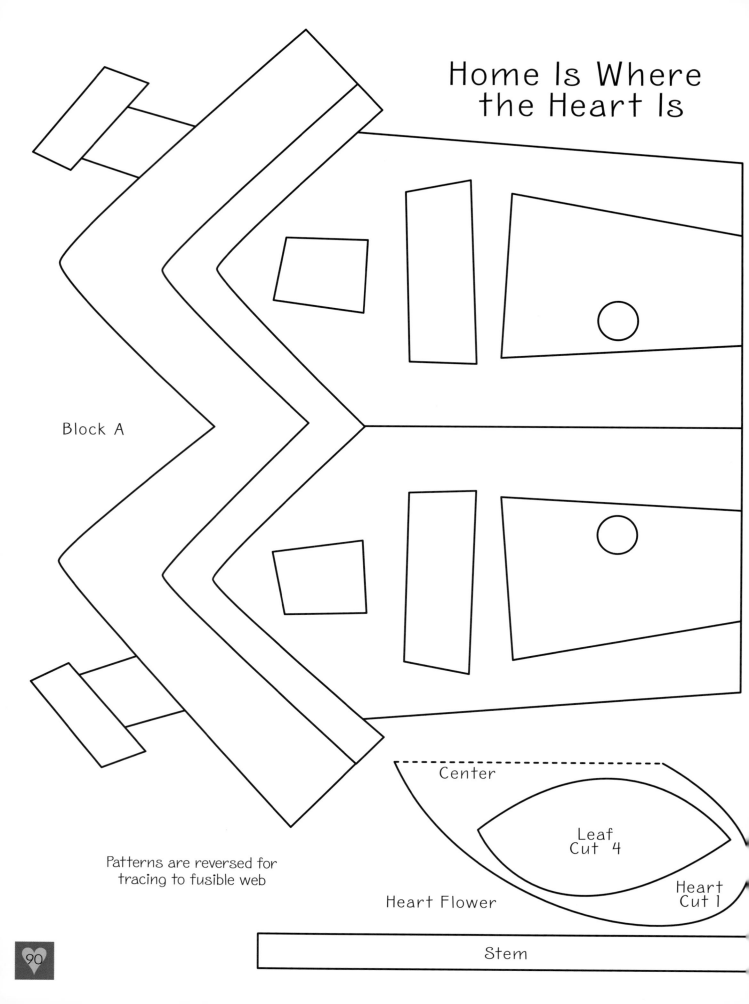

Home Is Where the Heart Is

Block A

Patterns are reversed for tracing to fusible web

Center

Leaf
Cut 4

Heart
Cut 1

Heart Flower

Stem

90

Alphabet
Soup

Patterns are reversed for
tracing to fusible web

91

Alphabet
Soup

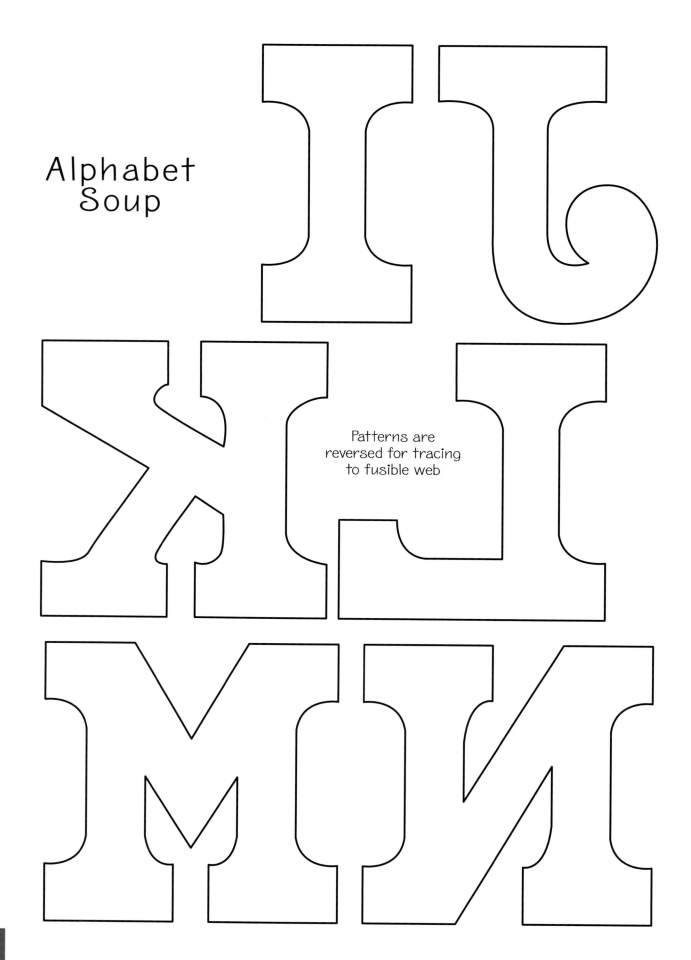

Patterns are
reversed for tracing
to fusible web

92

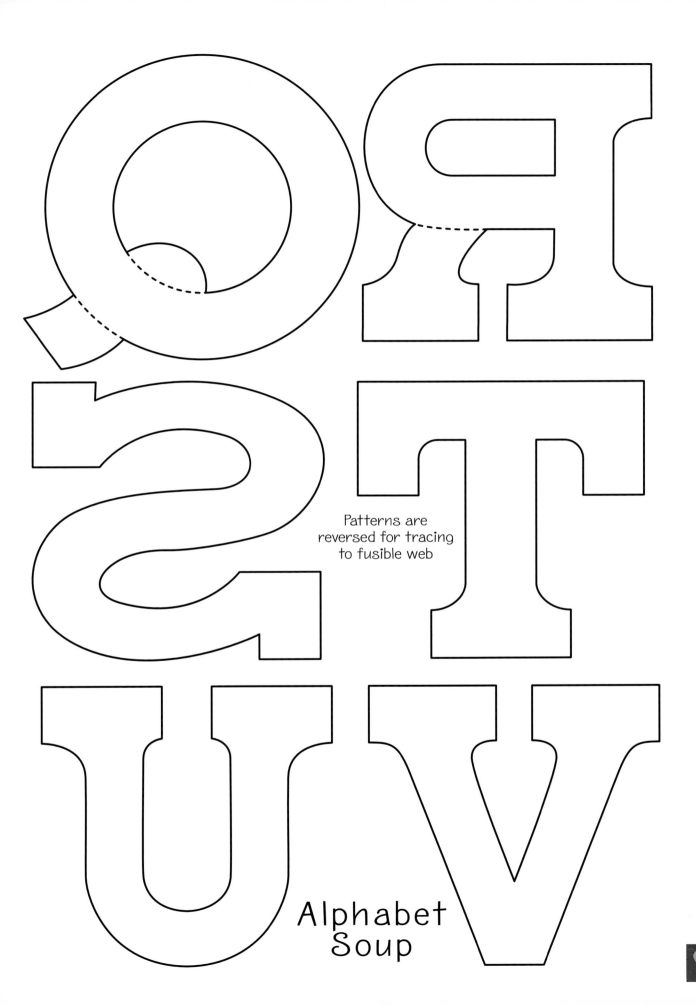

Patterns are
reversed for tracing
to fusible web

Alphabet
Soup

Alphabet Soup

Patterns are reversed for tracing to fusible web

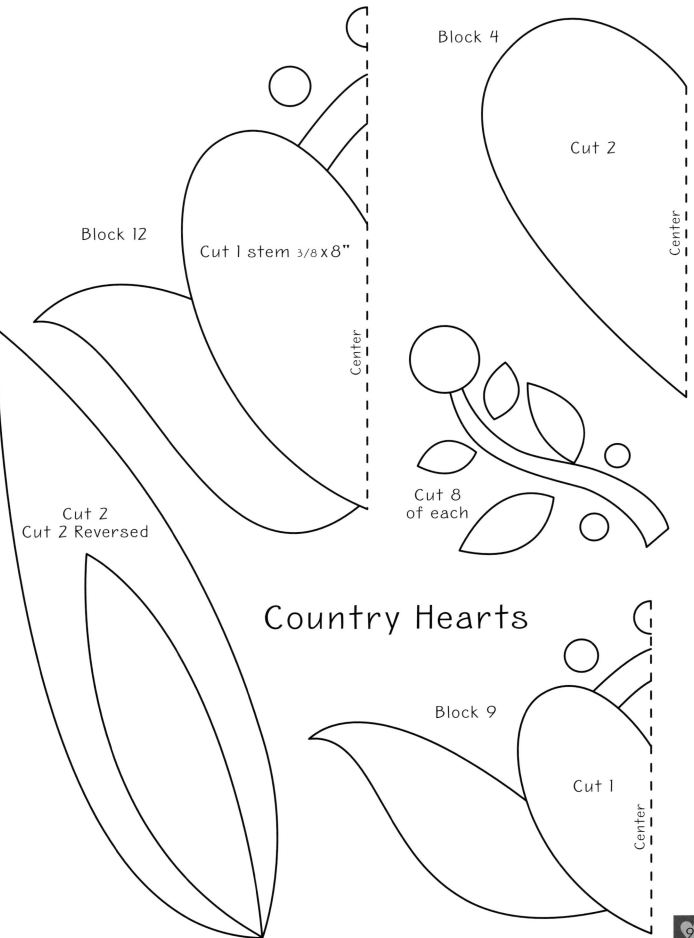

Block 4

Cut 2

Center

Block 12

Cut 1 stem 3/8 x 8"

Center

Cut 2
Cut 2 Reversed

Cut 8
of each

Country Hearts

Block 9

Cut 1

Center

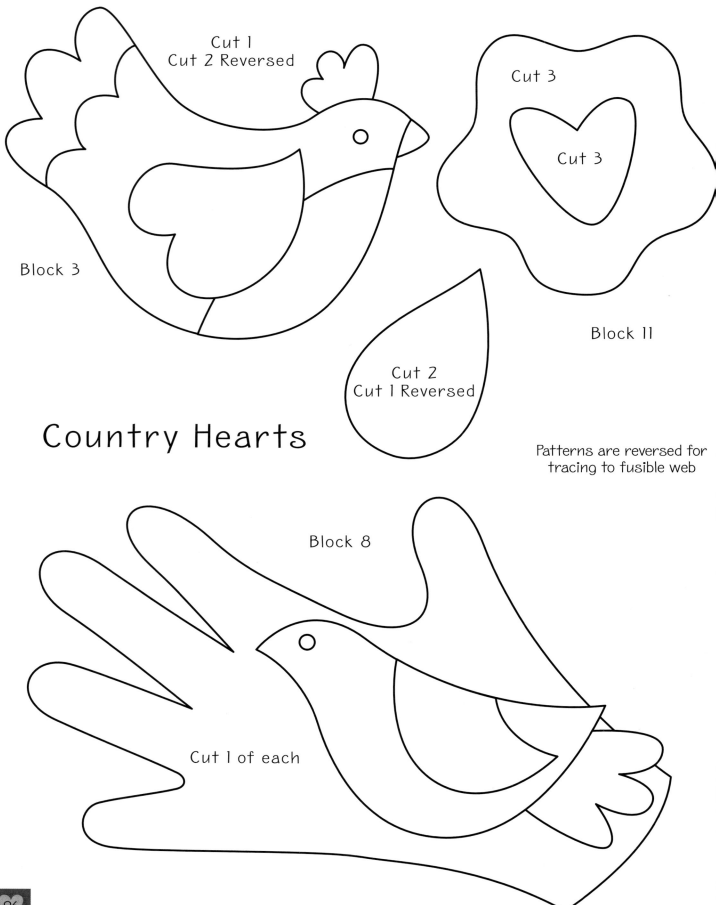

Cut 1
Cut 2 Reversed

Cut 3

Cut 3

Block 3

Block 11

Cut 2
Cut 1 Reversed

Country Hearts

Patterns are reversed for tracing to fusible web

Block 8

Cut 1 of each

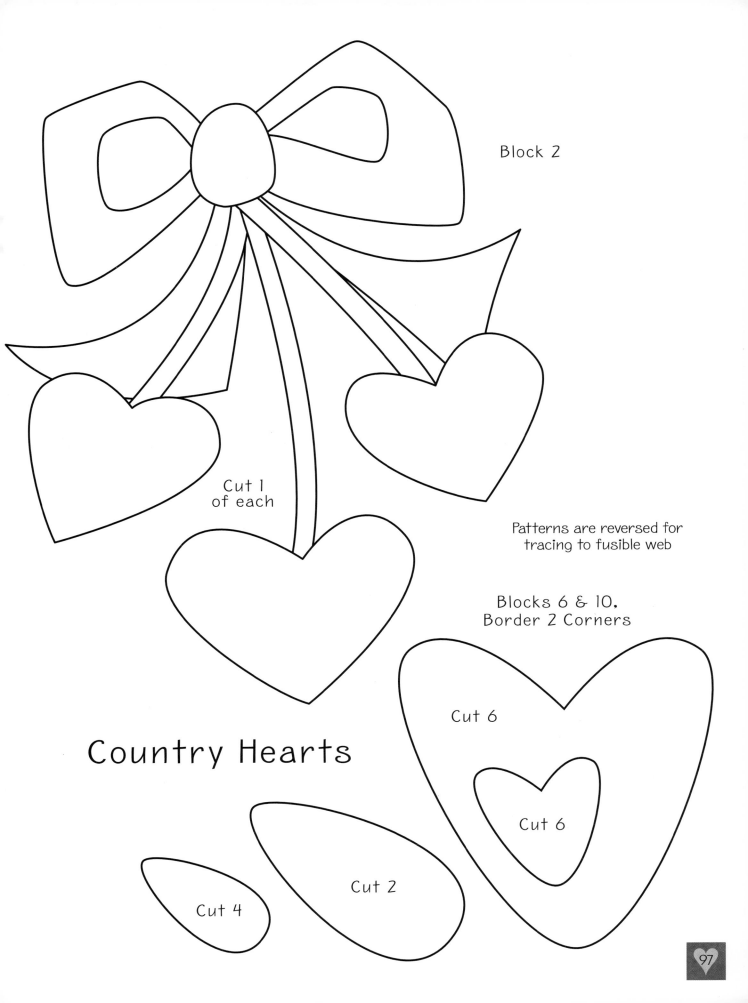

Block 2

Cut 1
of each

Patterns are reversed for
tracing to fusible web

Blocks 6 & 10,
Border 2 Corners

Country Hearts

Cut 6

Cut 6

Cut 2

Cut 4

Country Hearts

Cut 1 of each

Block 5

Patterns are reversed for
tracing to fusible web

Country
Hearts

Match to dotted line on page 98 for full pattern

Cut 1 of each

Block 1

Block 5

Patterns are reversed for
tracing to fusible web

99

Country Hearts

Cut 1 of each

Block 7

Patterns are reversed for
tracing to fusible web

Conversation Hearts

Base Square

Make a 150% copy for full-sized pattern.
Permission granted to photocopy for individual use.

Patterns are reversed for
tracing to fusible web

Conversation Hearts

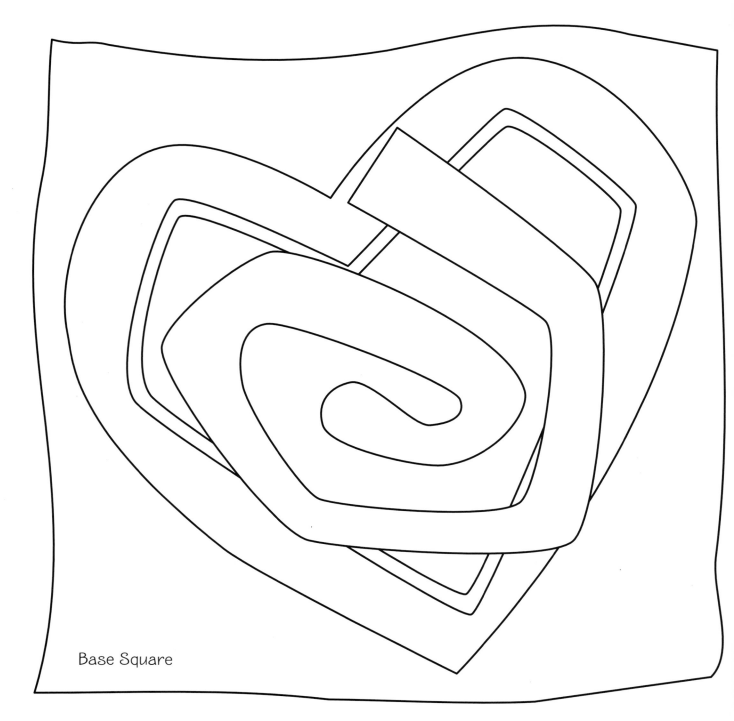

Base Square

Make a 150% copy for full-sized pattern.
Permission granted to photocopy for individual use.

102

Patterns are reversed for
tracing to fusible web